Motivational Management

Inspiring Your People for Maximum Performance

ALEXANDER HIAM

AMACOM
American Management Association
New York • Atlanta • Brussels • Buenos Aires • Chicago • London • Mexico City
San Francisco • Shanghai • Tokyo • Toronto • Washington, D.C.

Special discounts on bulk quantities of AMACOM books are available to corporations, professional associations, and other organizations. For details, contact Special Sales Department, AMACOM, *a division of American Management Association*, 1601 Broadway, New York, NY 10019. Tel.: 212-903-8316. Fax: 212-903-8083. Web site: www.amacombooks.org

This publication is designed to provide accurate and authoritative information in regard to the subject matter covered. It is sold with the understanding that the publisher is not engaged in rendering legal, accounting, or other professional service. If legal advice or other expert assistance is required, the services of a competent professional person should be sought.

Library of Congress Cataloging-in-Publication Data

Hiam, Alexander.
   Motivational management : inspiring your people for maximum performance / Alexander Hiam.
        p.   cm.
   Includes bibliographical references and index.
   ISBN 0-8144-0738-2
   1. Employee motivation.   2. Personnel management.   I. Title.
HF5549.5.M63 H52 2003
658.3'14—dc21   2002007305

Printing number

10 9 8 7 6 5 4 3 2 1

Contents

Introduction

Managers have a tough job. By definition, they must accomplish their goals and do their work *through the work of others*. The old saying that "If you want something done right, do it yourself" has a ring of truth to it, because it is usually harder to get employees to do a challenging job well than to do it yourself. Yet managers must let go of their own urge to just step in and make things right, and they must instead nurture the necessary competencies and commitment in their employees.

Achieving difficult goals through the work of others is of course an age-old challenge. Whoever built the pyramids must have wrestled with it. But in some ways, the challenge is a new one for us today. As we'll explore in Chapter 1, managers now face challenges that need a lot more effort, creative problem-solving, and willingness to change than did the previous generation of managers. As I visit workplaces and speak to audiences of managers and executives, I hear a common set of frustrations and desires having to do with the need to achieve tough and variable goals in a tough and variable world. To be better and quicker and smarter as an organization requires us to be better and quicker and smarter as *individuals*. That means everyone, not just the managers. How do we achieve that goal?

Some of the traditional answers still apply. Managers need to have appropriate strategies to implement. They need to be sincere and dedicated. But many of the other answers are changing because the results we need are changing.

We are not building old-fashioned pyramids. We cannot define work as the repetitive cutting and carrying of blocks of stone for decades at a time.

Our pyramids have to be finished this quarter and every block of stone needs to be made out of new composite materials and then custom-fitted by teams of employees who, incidentally, have never done this job before and who don't have enough tools or time to implement the blueprint the manager is looking at. Now what? Well, we could tell the employees to work faster. And if that doesn't do the trick, we could threaten to fire the slowest. Wait a second, that sounds a bit too negative. Let's organize them into teams, then add a prize for the fastest team. Will that work? Will we have the best new pyramid in the shortest length of time for the least cost? The answer is still likely to be no.

The kind of solutions I just described to the pyramid-building puzzle are examples of applying what I call level-one management to a level-two problem. Level-one management uses traditional top-down, command-and-control methods to structure and routinize and direct the work. It's great in a stable, relatively predictable environment.

A level-two strategic environment is harder to predict and faster changing. It requires a creative, entrepreneurial (opportunity-making) approach on the part of the organization, which of course means that managers need different sorts of qualities from their employees. But we can't simply begin importing superhumans from another planet; we still have the same sorts of people in our workforce. In many cases, we need to generate new and different types of performance from the exact same individuals. How do we get level-two performances out of our employees instead of level-one performances? *Something* has to change.

And the something that has to change is *us*, the managers. We need a new approach, a new set of tools and techniques. And we are working on this challenge. Many new approaches are developed and tried every year. Most organizations are in transition right now, with a mix of management methods and strategic approaches, some of which are clearly operating at level two. To be an effective manager today means helping with this transition. Ideally, it means leading the way by developing and adopting new management approaches that naturally generate the kinds of performances needed for strategic success. This book is intended to aid any manager who is eager to take up this challenge.

I named my most recent book *Making Horses Drink* after the old saying that you can lead a horse to water, but you can't make it drink. There are also some—perhaps many—things you cannot simply tell employees to do or make your organization do just by commanding them to happen. As we move toward level-two management, we bump into more and more of these things that require special inspiration, that don't just happen because somebody wrote a memo ordering them to be done.

Traditional command-and-control management will not generate the kinds of performances we most need from our employees today, as we will see in Chapters 1 and 2. We need employees who are self-motivated and eager to take initiative to address our challenging performance requirements. We need a turned-on, fast-learning workforce. We need our organization to be thirsty for change, willing to try harder, and eager to succeed. My goal as an author, consultant, and trainer is to help managers achieve exceptional performance in this new, challenging level-two environment. In this book, I'll share many of the tools and techniques that my firm uses to help managers achieve this important and difficult requirement.

Motivational Management

CHAPTER 1

The Quest for Star Performers

I've tried to create a culture of caring
for people in the totality of their
lives, not just at work. There's no
magic formula. It's like building a
giant mosaic—it takes thousands of
little pieces.

—Herb Kelleher, CEO, Southwest
Airlines

Just like Herb Kelleher, you too need to create a positive, can-
do culture that, as he describes it, gives people "the license
to be themselves." Because, as Kelleher observed, "the intangibles
are more important than the tangibles. Someone can go out and
buy airplanes from Boeing and ticket counters, but they can't buy
our culture, our esprit de corps."

Kelleher is talking about the differences between a workplace
where everyone goes through the motions (like cogs in a machine)
and a workplace where people are turned on and eager to perform
well, individually and as a group. He is talking about the difference
between a workplace where employees feel that they are expected
to "check their brains at the gate" and one in which their ideas and
enthusiasms are welcomed and harnessed to meaningful goals.

The difference can be bigger than we generally recognize, which
is why I'm so excited about the chance to explore this issue with

1

you in the coming pages. Companies with that special spirit Kelleher speaks of can and do outperform their rivals. Supervisors, managers, or team leaders who nurture that special something in their group tend not only to achieve more but to find it a heck of a lot more fun and rewarding to go to work each day—as do their people. The intangibles, as Kelleher calls them, are increasingly important in the workplace today.

> "I always thought the company wanted me to leave my brain at the gate."
> (Employee of an auto manufacturer, quoted in the *London Times.*)

Managing for the New Work Environment

Do you need employees who check their brains at the entrance and just do what you tell them until the clock says they can go? Probably not. Most managers feel that they need a far higher level of involvement—that the kind of challenges they face require a far more dedicated and involved employee than this old stereotype suggests.

Work is harder than, or at least different from, how it used to be, and we increasingly need the full involvement of employees. To be successful we need not only their hands, but also their ideas and enthusiasms. There is a big difference between the results you get when employees perform well and fully, and when they just go through the motions. Brian McQuaid, executive director of human resources at MCI, told *The Wall Street Journal* that new employees only accomplish 60 percent of what experienced employees do (the firm compared employees who had been there less than three months with those who had been there longer). Even more striking, customer satisfaction was measurably lower for these less expert new employees than for others. Combine these findings with the observation that a 5 percent drop in overall employee efficiency cuts annual revenue by "a couple of hundred million dollars" at

MCI, according to McQuaid, and the links from how individual employees perform to how the company performs become clearer.

McQuaid also reports that measures of employee satisfaction are linked at MCI to both customer satisfaction and employee productivity—key indicators of both quality and quantity of work performed (from a syndicated story in *The Wall Street Journal*, February 7, 1999). So, at MCI at least, employees who perform their work well, not just adequately, can make all the difference between success and failure for the company as a whole.

A Hypothetical Challenge

Imagine that you have been asked to select a boat and crew to do a specific job. Your job is to load large bales of hay and take them across a wide, calm, slow-moving river every day. What kind of boat and crew do you want for this job? Select one from the following options:

▶ *Option A*. A large, easy-to-load barge and a crew that is disciplined and good at doing repetitive work consistently

▶ *Option B*. A fast, seaworthy sailboat with a crew of intelligent, experienced sailors who are able to do a wide variety of things well, depending upon the situation

Option A makes good sense for the job you have been given. You don't need speed or flexibility, you simply need something that can carry the same heavy load across the same flat water again and again. And if your workers want to "leave their brains at the gate" and do their work mindlessly, so what—the work we're talking about here is pretty mindless, if truth be told.

But now imagine a different situation and see which option you'd prefer. Imagine you have been asked to head out to sea in storm season to try to find and rescue a missing ship that was carrying an important delegation with a load of treasure. Now which of the options do you choose, the barge and routine-oriented crew in

Option A or the fast sailing ship and flexible, intelligent crew in Option B?

Managing in Stormy Weather

As a manager today, you face challenges that are unique. Studies of businesses and their competitive environments show that almost every organization faces challenges that are different from those of earlier decades. Things change faster. There are more potential competitors and customers. Technology dishes up more frequent surprises. It is harder to see the future and more important than ever to be creative and innovative—in other words, to help shape the future rather than to assume the past will continue as is.

All these challenges combine to create a business environment that demands a fast pace of change and frequent innovations on the part of employees and their organizations. No matter the size or type of organization, it must behave in innovative ways, seeking opportunities, solving problems, and embracing new directions. This need for agility and intelligence is as urgent in a government agency or nonprofit as it is in a for-profit company. There is emerging now a general set of requirements for organizations, their managers, and their employees that includes attributes like initiative, flexibility, and creative problem-solving.

In a traditional, stable environment, managers are protectors of the status quo. Their role is to make sure employees understand and follow the established procedures, because these procedures reflect many years of testing and refinement and are probably better than anything that employees could come up with independently. But today's working environment is rarely stable, and the nature of work is different and the role of the manager must shift in response.

In today's turbulent, fast-changing environment, managers are constructive enemies of the status quo. They need to create a healthy momentum by stimulating employees to innovate and change. Their role is to bring out the natural enthusiasm and intelligence of their people and make sure they apply it to their work.

There are far fewer layers of hierarchy today, because hierarchy gets in the way of innovation and fast response. There is less supporting staff for managers because secretaries and personal assistants are a luxury that few organizations can now afford. And so individual managers generally supervise more people with fewer resources than their counterparts did in earlier decades. And since most managers have plenty of work on their own desks, they must manage their people in between trying to get their *own* work done.

Rekindling Trust

According to the massive General Social Survey of the National Opinion Research Center at the University of Chicago, people in the United States are gradually becoming less trusting of each other. In response to the question, "Do you think people would try to take advantage of you if they got a chance, or would they try to be fair?" a healthy majority used to vote for "fair," but this trusting view has been slipping down steadily. In the 1970s, 64 percent thought others would be fair. In the 1980s, that percentage slipped to 58 percent, and by the end of the 1990s it was down to 52 percent. One possible explanation is that there are new values in the younger cohorts taking over the workplace, but whatever the reason it behooves business leaders to keep this shift in mind.[1]

An obvious implication is that *your employees are less likely than ever to trust you to be doing the right thing*—so you better tell them what you are doing and give them enough information to reach a favorable conclusion on their own. Perhaps the rise of mistrust explains why there has been an increase in how important management communications and information-sharing are viewed in surveys of employee opinion.

Here's a related question from the same General Social Survey that is perhaps even more telling: "Would you say that most of the time people try to be helpful, or that they are just looking out for themselves?" In the 1970s, a majority—59 percent—voted for "helpful." Now the number has slipped below half, to 48 percent. In other words, probably more than half of your

U.S. employees believe that the people around them are just looking out for themselves. This means that whenever two or more people are interacting in their work, they are probably distrustful of each other's motives. In that context, you can see why it is necessary to work on building trust and emphasizing strong communications and teamwork in the workplace.

The Employee's Challenging Work Environment

The employees you supervise today also work in an environment that differs significantly from their traditional environment. The nature of their work is far more variable—the typical employee sees frequent changes in the goals, in the processes and technologies, and in the work assignments. The workforce is more diverse (as are the customers). And employees' work often takes them across functional and organizational boundaries. They may need to negotiate or collaborate with people from other functions and departments on a daily or weekly basis. They may be members of teams that include people from many other areas of their organization or even from separate businesses.

There is also growing evidence to suggest that today's employees are expected to be more productive—to work harder and longer and produce more for less—than their counterparts of a decade or more ago. In fact, productivity goes up a little bit every year in the United States (and also in Canada and many European countries), which means that employees are somehow managing to produce more than ever before for each hour or day they work. To maintain this momentum, they cannot continue to work as they have before. They have to work harder or (preferably) smarter in order to be more productive each month and year.

Add to this the reality that today's employees face frequent challenges and changes. They must often adjust to changes at work, including occasional downsizing and reorganization, new technologies and systems, and new products and customers. The composition of any workplace is also changing faster than ever before.

Employee turnover is up, and it is common for personnel changes to disrupt a smoothly functioning team or work group. Each time a new coworker or manager arrives, there is a period of adjustment for the rest of the group. And then it happens all over again.

It is no wonder that employees today report high levels of work-related stress, sleeplessness, and anxiety about their work. (For instance, according to a recent survey, 39 percent of employees say they often or always find their work stressful.) Negative feelings such as these interfere with performance on the job and they lower employees' enthusiasm and commitment for what they are doing.

Employees' attitudes and especially their level of motivation—or overall enthusiasm for doing their work well—are a growing concern for all managers. In fact, whether employees even *trust* their managers, employer, and each other is an issue in many workplaces today. There are two reasons for this:

1. Today's fast-changing, challenging work environment is more likely to create negative feelings, such as stress and frustration, and therefore poses a constant threat to healthy work attitudes.

2. The need for creative problem-solving and rapid adjustment to change means that employees must be more self-motivated than ever before. Regimented, obedient employees do not succeed in today's challenging environment. Managers depend on employee initiative, enthusiasm, and commitment more than ever.

I see a widespread acceptance in the business world of the need for new and different business strategies—the organizational level of response to the changing business environment. But I do not see as clear an understanding of the need for a response at the level of the individual employees and their supervisors and work groups. Yet the responsibility for producing new, more flexible, and adaptable corporate strategies falls in the end to individual employees taking a more flexible and adaptable approach to their work.

Changing Views of the Ideal Employee

As a result of these workplace trends, the manager's "ideal employees" today are very different from what they once were. But people are essentially the same. So to generate the kind of employee behavior you need to succeed today as a manager, you need to manage employees differently. You need to recognize that you are on the frontier of an effort to redesign the field of management and to reinvent work itself.

This book on motivational management is intended to help you acquire the skills needed to succeed as an innovative manager and to help your people succeed in today's turbulent and challenging work environment. I want to ask you to roll up your sleeves for a moment and take a more active role in this quest by doing a quick activity that I often start out with when I present to a live audience in a workshop.

Exercise 1-1. Describe your ideal employees.

What kind of behavior do you want to see in your employees? To succeed as a manager and to help your organization achieve its goals, what kind of employees do you need? Take a moment to create a list of descriptive words or phrases:

My ideal employees are:

What did you come up with in the exercise? Whatever your list, you need to recognize that how you manage your people will determine in large part whether they fit your ideal profile or not. In this book you'll learn methods that can help you manage for many of the characteristics that most managers say they want and need in their employees today.

When I do this same exercise in live courses with groups of managers, I keep seeing terms on their lists like self-sufficient, motivated, take initiative, problem-solvers, good communicators, good listeners, fast learners, helpful, resourceful, team players, careful, creative, and (especially) responsible.

Did you come up with any of these words or ones that mean the same thing? I imagine you probably did, and even if you didn't list all of them you may find them appropriate now that you see them written down. These are the kinds of characteristics most managers want and need in their employees today.

And what don't they want? What characteristics are the ones managers want to avoid in their people? Again, you can think about this yourself. It makes an interesting exercise.

Exercise 1-2. Describe bad employee behavior.

List the characteristics that might make an employee difficult to manage:

Bad behaviors are:

What did you come up with? If your list is similar to ones I see in live courses, I think it will include phrases like the following:

Doing the least amount needed instead of the most

Not caring, not being helpful or concerned

Having a bad attitude and low motivation

Not learning

Not taking responsibility

Making too many mistakes

Working too slowly

Coming late and leaving early

Complaining

Griping

Refusing to take on responsibilities

Resisting your efforts to manage them

Forcing you to use high-pressure techniques to make them do their work.

Manager don't want to feel like they are always pushing employees uphill. Nobody wants to deal with surly, uncooperative employees who resist our efforts to lead them and who take no personal interest in achieving the organization's vital goals. People who are just in it for themselves are a nightmare to manage. They don't care about the work of the organization. They can be *cynical, impolite, and uncooperative*. They only work for what they can get out of it, and the less they work the better.

What every manager wants is:

▶ Enthusiastic, motivated employees who believe in the work and in their ability to succeed in doing it

▶ Employees who are a pleasure to manage because they are eager to move ahead

▶ Employees who make it easy to manage them because they are eager to collaborate with you in pursuit of improved performance

▶ Employees who pitch in and help whenever there is a problem instead of complaining and waiting for you to solve it for them.

In today's challenging workplace, it is more vital than ever for managers to have employees who fit this ideal. There is just not time or money to waste on dragging anyone around who is determined to be a dead weight in the organization.

Internal vs. External Motivation

Frederick Herzberg, a leading expert on the psychology of motivation in the workplace, points out the importance of one's own internal motivation when he says, "I can charge a man's battery, then recharge it, and recharge it again. But it is only when he has his own generator that we can talk about motivation. He then needs no outside stimulation. He wants to do it." As the manager of others, you definitely do not want to feel like you are having to pour your own energy into them all the time to keep them going. You'd far rather have them operating off the energy they generate internally!

What most managers want today is employees who are internally—or to use the technical term, *intrinsically*—motivated to do their jobs well. *Intrinsic motivation* is motivation that arises from within. Intrinsically motivated employees are enthusiastic and eager to succeed, and they bring their own motivation to the work at hand. As a manager, you don't have to force them to do their work. They *want* to do it and they want to do it well.

The Self-Motivated Employee

Intrinsic motivation generates the kind of behaviors managers look for in their ideal employee. People who are intrinsically motivated to do their work are enthusiastic, responsible, caring, and eager to improve. They don't always watch the clock. They are happy to help someone else out, to contribute to a team, or to take on a little extra responsibility themselves if need be. They look to their managers to support them and help them get the information and resources needed to do a good job. But they don't expect their managers to motivate them. When you manage intrinsically motivated people, you don't have to be constantly pushing them uphill. They *want* to go—they just need a little help and direction to make sure they go the right way.

The typical description of poor employees does not fit this picture of intrinsic motivation at all. Instead, it describes people who probably have little of their own enthusiasm for their work, if any, and who only act out of necessity when external factors force them to. As a manager, you may find yourself in the role of one of those external factors that forces these employees to work—but you won't enjoy the role!

Managing people based on extrinsic motivation is a thankless task. You have to keep providing external pressures to make them perform. You can hold threats over them, you can offer rewards for performance, or you can try any combination of both. But however you do it, you are providing all the motivation and they are doing what you want only because that is how they can earn the reward or avoid the punishment.

When you turn your back for even a moment, extrinsically motivated employees will stop working. They will come in late and do less on days when you aren't there to watch them. They will try to sneak out of work or do a poor job when they think you won't notice. Pilferage and dishonesty are common among such employees too. And you will always feel like you have to work extra hard just to keep them working at all. That is because extrinsically motivated employees tend to resist your efforts to push them to higher levels of performance. You push and pull, they resist.

Not much fun for you as a manager. So when we talk of motivational management in this book, we aren't talking about extrinsic motivation. We are talking about managing for high levels of intrinsic motivation. The goal is to turn your people on and stimulate their natural drive to perform their work well, succeed in their careers, and help your organization succeed too.

Exercise 1-3. Assessing intrinsic and extrinsic motivation levels.

Here is a tool you can use to decide to what extent employees are intrinsically and/or extrinsically motivated. If you currently manage a group of employees, apply it to them. Circle "yes" or "no" for each of the twelve statements depending on which answer you think is more accurate.

These employees . . .	Circle the best answer. (Be careful: The placement of "yes" and "no" options changes from question to question.)	
1. Wait for their manager to tell them what to do.	Yes	No
2. Help each other out whenever necessary.	No	Yes
3. Often volunteer for extra work.	No	Yes
4. Work hardest when a supervisor is watching.	Yes	No
5. Come up with lots of ways to improve their work.	No	Yes
6. Complain frequently.	Yes	No
7. Act like it's "us against them."	Yes	No
8. Feel bad if they make a mistake.	No	Yes
9. Ask for new challenges.	No	Yes
10. Work hardest when they are offered special rewards.	Yes	No
11. Often need to be told to get going.	Yes	No

12. Encourage each other.	No	Yes
Total number circled in each column:		
The higher the number, the more important that type of motivation is right now for these employees:	Extrinsic motivation score	Intrinsic motivation score

Which column has the highest score? That score tells you what kind of motivation dominates in the group of employees right now. If extrinsic motivation dominates, they are motivated more by external pressures than by self-motivation. If the intrinsic score is higher, then this group of employees is predominantly self-motivated. The way in which groups of employees are supervised and their work is structured can have a strong influence on their scores on this assessment, and in later chapters we will discuss methods designed to maximize the intrinsic motivation score and de-emphasize extrinsic motivation.

You can use this assessment as a management tool in the future. Check your employees' scores periodically on it as you practice the motivational management methods in this course. Try to move toward a perfect score of 0/12, where all your circled answers are in the right-hand *Intrinsic Motivation* column.

Ask Permission to Give Negative Feedback

How you use each interaction with employees is an important element of motivational management. Each opportunity to interact with them can be harnessed to the goal of awakening their internal motivation. For instance, before you give someone bad news, negative feedback, or out-and-out criticism, consider asking their permission. It's polite. Tactful. Considerate. And those are three things most employees say their leaders aren't.

How do you ask permission? There are a number of ways. The simplest way is to say, "Can I give you some feedback?" or words to that effect. "Can I say something?" is more vague, but many people recognize it is a prelude to criticism and so it can work well too.

Even more polite is to give them control over *when* to give the feedback, as in "I've got some feedback I'd like to give you. When would be a good time to talk about it?" or "Is this an okay time?"

You might also consider giving them control over *where and even how* you give the feedback, as in, "Can we talk here or is there somewhere else you'd prefer?" and "Would you like me to talk to you about it or would you prefer an e-mail that you can respond to later?" This permits employees to manage their own bad news. Some people get tense when receiving critical input and would rather not have to do it face-to-face. And some people prefer to do it quickly and informally in an open or even public area, while others prefer to find a quiet, private place and a formal setting.

Summary

When you manage to maximize intrinsic motivation, you get self-motivated employees who are eager to perform well and believe in the importance of their work. All you have to do is help them achieve the high levels of performance they desire. That is an ideal way to manage in today's workplace. But in many cases, managers find themselves dealing with groups of employees who are in the habit of working more out of extrinsic than intrinsic motivation. This habit has been reinforced by their previous managers and by the systems within which they work. And it can lead to a pattern of resistance in which employees view their work *and* their managers negatively and are suspicious of your efforts to introduce changes and improvements.

In the next chapter, we will look at what happens when negative attitudes contaminate motivation and turn off employees' intrinsic motivation entirely. This situation can occur for many reasons, and it leads to negative attitudes that are difficult to change and to job performances that are surprisingly resistant to your efforts to improve or modify them. The result is a frustrating employee relationship that leads many managers to be stricter with employees—which unfortunately only compounds the problem.

One of the most important elements of motivational management is the creation of a positive, can-do emotional climate as a backdrop to specific goals and tasks. Intrinsic motivation flourishes in the right emotional climate, and withers in the wrong one, so this is a good foundational issue to work on in trying to turn on employees' natural motivation to achieve and succeed in their work. And there are a number of other levers the leader can turn to that are often different from what we traditionally think of as management tools—but we'll take this point up in Chapter 2.

Notes

1. See Geoffrey Meredith et. al., *Managing by Defining Moments* (New York: John Wiley & Sons, 2002).

CHAPTER 2

Creating a
Positive Performance
Environment

This book will show you many tools and techniques for maximizing internal motivation. But the thing is, nobody is going to adopt new management behaviors unless there is a real need—in particular, a need to *replace other behaviors* because they are no longer effective. So let's think for a minute about what managers commonly do, about the current menu of leadership behaviors. Some of the traditional manager's performance levers have their far end embedded in employees' extrinsic motivation, not their intrinsic motivation—so we want to make sure we know which ones NOT to use.

Avoiding Demotivational Management

Here are some things that we have all seen over and over in workplaces—but that we want to try to avoid in the future. Why avoid these behaviors? Because they may generate increased effort in the short term, but they do it only by forcing performance through external leverage, and this happens at the expense of internal initiative. So try to avoid the following common actions:

▶ Raising your voice to show employees you are irritated or angry about their performance

► Threatening to withhold resources or opportunities

► Warning employees that you are going to "review the troops" or otherwise check their work and they better be ready (or else)

► Stepping up your micro-management of employees by giving lots of specific instructions and directions

► Correcting employees frequently with negative feedback

► Taking work away from people who aren't doing it quickly or well

► Giving duplicate assignments to more than one person or team to make sure at least someone produces the work you need on time (and thereby generating competition between the workers or teams)

► Putting the loudest, most assertive and directive person in charge of a shift, team, or project to make sure it gets done

► Nagging employees with questions about whether or when they are going to finish something

► Avoiding regular interactions with employees about their work unless something is going wrong

Here's the fun thing about compiling such a list of what not to do. When people look at the list, they often realize that it pretty much exhausts the options that are commonly used to try to get employees to perform better. These are not only widespread management ploys, they are for many managers a general menu of options. People say things like, "If I can't do any of those things when my employees perform below par, then what can I do? You're tying both hands behind my back!"

Well, to be honest, that is the point. If you are managing with your hands, then maybe it would be better to switch to managing with your head. At least that's what I'm tempted to say in reply.

Usually I am more polite and just say that I'll show people a bunch of other options to replace these ones—options that evoke employees' intrinsic motivation instead of just poking them with extrinsic motivational sticks. Because clearly the alternative to that list of traditional levers is *not* to simply do nothing. Managers need to be active in their relationships with their employees; they can't ignore them. But management actions need to be guided by a clear understanding of the new performance requirements and the need to use motivational methods appropriate to these new requirements.

Which Path Are Your Employees On?

When employees are managed in the heavy-handed and relatively insensitive manner that is traditional in most workplaces (and that produces actions such those listed above), the employees often feel irritated or frustrated with their managers. They may also feel angry, mistreated, underappreciated, or stressed. In other words, employees often *walk around with negative feelings* because of their interactions with their managers. (This is, I think, one of the dirty little secrets of the modern workplace. Nobody likes to admit that managers and supervisors often turn off their employees as an accidental side effect of their efforts to lead them!)

Exhibit 2-1 illustrates a view of employee behavior based on the idea that we all respond to stimuli—events in our lives or in our work—*differently,* depending on how we feel at the time.

This is an important point because it runs counter to the traditional behaviorist view we may have been taught in school or in a college psychology class. Traditionally, most scientists look at behavior as arising consistently in a relatively mechanical way in response to a stimulus. The idea that people might process that stimulus differently depending on their frame of mind is at odds with this mechanistic tradition—and yet very much consistent with what we really see in the workplace and in life in general. The old question about whether the glass is half empty or half full captures this idea that you can look at a stimulus two different ways depending on whether

EXHIBIT 2-1. Two paths.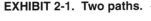

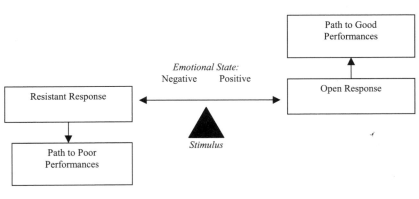

you are in an up or down mood. We know this is true—we just need to incorporate this truth into our management behavior in order to profit from it.

For simplicity, the diagram in Exhibit 2-1 distinguishes between only two broad categories of feelings: good (or positive) and bad (or negative). We can (and later will) differentiate further within these categories, but it is not important to do so right now.

Positive feelings are any feelings that lead us to feel up: happy, enthusiastic, confident, pleased, proud, optimistic, or any other emotional state that feels good. Negative feelings are any that lead us to feel down, and can include feelings like unhappiness, stress, anger, sorrow, depression, and pessimism. Depending on whether we are in a positive or negative emotional state, we react to stimuli very differently.

Specifically, employees who are in an up, positive emotional state are likely to view challenges as opportunities. And they are likely to be self-motivated (intrinsically motivated) to take on those challenges. So their emotional state is one of the determinants of whether they will be intrinsically motivated to do their work or not.

To make the switch from extrinsic to intrinsic motivators, managers need to (among other things) attend more carefully to the emotional state of their employees. Let's explore this idea with a simple management case history.

A CASE IN POINT

Juanita is the newly appointed manager of a large bookstore in a success-ful national chain. She has several dozen employees working at her loca-tion in a variety of positions, from the front registers to the back room and from the coffee bar to special events. Juanita previously worked as assis-tant manager in another store in the same chain, where she and her boss oversaw a redecoration of the store and the introduction of twice-weekly Meet-the-Author evenings that proved very popular and attracted lots of customers. Juanita was asked to take over a store that was not doing very well. She is expected to turn the store around by overseeing another re-decoration and introducing meet-the-author evenings and other events.

But Juanita is frustrated at her lack of progress. The employees at her store do not seem to share her enthusiasm. Every time she tries to intro-duce a new idea, they act as if she is trying to make their lives more diffi-cult. She has held several staff meetings, where she explained that management wants the store to increase its sales and begin to use new ideas from other more successful stores. She expected the employees to be excited about the opportunity to turn the store around, since the alterna-tive would be that headquarters would close them down. But instead of embracing the opportunity, they seem to do everything they can to mess it up.

And now Juanita feels like the problem has really come to a head. She advertised the first Meet-the-Author night and scheduled it for this evening, assigning different employees the jobs of lining up food and drink, ordering copies of the author's books, and rearranging the store for the author's book signing and talk. But when she checked in with her employees this morning, no one had done a thing!

Juanita called several other stores in a panic and got hold of extra copies of the author's books, then drove all over the area to pick them up. While driving, she used her cell phone to call caterers and arranged for a last-minute order of finger foods to be delivered, since the manager of her store's snack bar had forgotten to prepare anything for the party and claimed that he didn't have any employees available to work a late shift. Then when Juanita finally got back to the store, she found that the day-shift employees had gone home without setting up the furniture for the event. There weren't enough people on the evening shift to do the setup, so Juanita set up folding chairs and tables and reorganized bookshelves by herself.

Somehow the event went well. She got a good turnout of customers, and the author was pleased. But Juanita realizes that she cannot continue to operate in this manner. She feels like telling her employees that they had better get with the program if they don't want to be fired, but she doesn't want to have to relate to them like that. At her old store, the managers and employees usually worked together as a team instead of working against each other. She wonders why this store is so much more difficult to manage than the other one and what she can do to turn employee attitudes around.

As you may have noticed, Juanita is experiencing the difference between her old group of employees who are on the motivation path and look at things positively, and her new group who are on the resistance path. They seem to have a negative perspective and, as a result, *respond to her initiatives as if they are problems instead of opportunities*. Unless she applies sufficient pressure, they will not do anything special to help her. But when she applies pressure, she is simply managing using extrinsic motivation—in other words, all the impetus comes from her and soon she will wear herself out with all that pushing.

Juanita's instinct is to get tough with her people, and that is perfectly understandable. But if you think about the model in Exhibit 2-1, you can see that *getting tough is not going to help her very much*. If her new employees are looking at things in a negative light, their basic emotional perspective is going to lead them to respond negatively to her efforts to motivate them. As long as they are on the resistance path, she will continue to struggle with them over performance issues. And she will continue to be frustrated in that her efforts to improve their performance don't seem to work. She may decide that she has bad employees, or she may lose confidence in herself as a manager.

The truth is that neither the employees nor the manager in this story are bad. They are just locked in a classic struggle that can*not* be fixed by focusing on performance issues, or even by applying incentives or other motivational influences. The underlying emotional framework has to be fixed first. Until Juanita's employees adopt a more positive view of their work, they will continue to prove difficult to manage. They will continue to view Juanita and her initiatives as irritants and problems, and they will continue to resist change to the extent they can get away with it. Juanita will find it a long, hard struggle trying to turn this store around unless she starts by turning the employees' attitudes around first.

Fixing the Emotional Frame

Juanita is going to have to focus on shifting employee attitudes from a negative to a positive starting framework before she can expect them to respond more positively to her management actions. She has to get them off the resistance path. To do so, she needs to use a variety of techniques that are covered in this book, including employing motivational communications—or communications with her employees that focus on stimulating a positive, self-motivated attitude. She is also going to need to apply her "emotional intelligence" or ability to understand and manage how people are feeling in her new workplace. These two approaches, covered in the next two chapters, will help her get employees off the resistance path and onto the path of positive self-motivation. Then she can begin to use new challenges to motivate her people—once they are in the right frame of mind to appreciate and embrace challenges instead of resisting them.

How will Juanita know that her efforts to move employees off the resistance path and onto the path of positive self-motivation are working? She will see a shift in their motivation, *from extrinsic to intrinsic*. So Juanita can track her progress by keeping an eye on the type of motivation that is predominating in her store. She could use Exercise 1-3 in Chapter 1 as a once-a-week check on her own progress.

Checking the Mirror: How Your Behavior Drives Their Attitudes

As a new manager, Juanita is at first going to think that she cannot control how her people feel. If the employees show up at her bookstore with negative attitudes and don't seem to take personal responsibility for making things better, what can *she* do about it? Managers can tell people what to *do*, but they can't tell them how to *feel*. In fact, some people would argue that it's none of the manager's business how employees feel about their work, as long as they do it. Their feelings are private and have nothing to do with their work.

Is a Poster Worth a Thousand Moods?

Many managers actually do try to tell employees exactly how to feel—and then get frustrated that the instructions were not followed. Perhaps you have seen some of those so-called motivational posters that are sold for use in the workplace, with pretty pictures from nature and a slogan at the bottom that tells people to be positive, cooperative, or motivated in their work.

Of course you don't change anyone's underlying frame of mind or mood simply by telling them to feel differently. Feelings are not under the verbal control of managers, let alone posters. But there is a misconception that you can actually take care of this responsibility for managing the emotional climate at work just by putting up a poster that tells people how to feel.

Although feelings may be private, they cannot be ignored by managers. The problem of course is that feelings have a powerful effect on performance, as the model in Exhibit 2-1 shows. You can see this effect most easily by thinking about your own behavior in different situations. Imagine how you would react in the following situation.

You work in a remote office of a large company. The site where you work is not considered important, and rumors keep surfacing that it will be closed down, but your boss will not discuss the rumors. Nobody at your site has had a raise in two years, but you just learned from a friend that employees at other locations of the company got a big raise recently. The office environment is depressing and uncomfortable. There is not enough space so everyone shares a cubicle with two other people. The building is shabby, and the equipment often breaks down.

Employees grumble about their work but most of them have been there so long they don't want to leave until they become eligible for retirement benefits. So they just do the minimum needed to get by and take as many sick days as they can get away with. You rarely speak one-on-one with your boss, but yesterday he called you into his office and assigned you to a new quality improvement team that is supposed to come up with ways to improve the quality and speed of your location's output. He said, "I know this is going to mean some extra work, but we have to do it—it's a companywide mandate. And I don't expect anyone will volunteer, so I'm going to assign the team members myself. I'll get back to you to let you know who else is on the team and when your first meeting will be."

How would you react to this assignment to a team project? Would you feel motivated, excited, and eager to get going? Or would you feel irritated, resentful, and resistant?

It is hard to imagine feeling positive about such an assignment, isn't it? There are too many things wrong with the situation. You probably have negative feelings about work and your workplace already, and so when your boss assigns you in this heavy-handed way to a project whose purpose is unclear and meaningless to you, you will not feel motivated by the challenge. In fact, you will dread the project and feel like you have an inconsiderate boss.

Some people are so naturally positive and optimistic that they are less affected by situations like these, while others are more pessimistic by nature and more easily affected. (We'll learn how to maximize optimism in our people in Chapters 5 and 9.) But everyone is affected to some degree, and the impact of the situation on their attitudes and feelings shapes how they respond to efforts to manage them.

The Feelings Paradox

As the case above illustrates, the feelings of employees have a huge impact on their behaviors in the workplace. Which is why you as a manager want and need to manage the emotional climate of your workplace. (In fact, if you think about it, motivation itself is nothing more or less than a feeling.) So you have an urgent need to manage feelings in order to manage performances.

On the other hand, there is the problem that you as a manager are not directly responsible for or in charge of your employees' emotional lives. Their feelings are truly their personal business and not something you as a manager have any specific right or authority to control. So what can you do? You want to make sure attitudes and feelings are positive, but you cannot exercise direct control over other people's feelings—and you probably wouldn't want to even if you could. It sounds kind of creepy and Big Brother-like to manage other people's feelings.

Managing the Factors You *Do* Control

This management paradox—the need to manage others' feelings about work and the impossibility and undesirability of doing so directly—can easily be resolved by recognizing that there are many things you already control as a manager that in turn affect your employees' feelings. You don't have to manage feelings directly. But you already do manage them indirectly. Most managers are unaware of the extent to which they set the emotional climate in their workplace.

The first and most powerful way in which you as a manager

affect employee attitudes and feelings is through your own feelings. What you feel has a powerful influence on the attitudes and feelings of your people. If you are emotionally very cool and detached, then you are creating a neutral emotional environment that discourages strong feelings of any kind, whether negative or positive. If you are optimistic and enthusiastic and view challenges with hope and excitement, this positive attitude can't help rubbing off on the people around you. If you are pessimistic, tired, stressed out, angry, or discouraged, these negative feelings can and do spread through your people.

The Good Humor Man

Herb Kelleher built Southwest into a major—and unusually profitable—airline, in part because of his constant good humor and willingness to find fun in his work—a positive attitude that has spread to others throughout his company. *The Wall Street Journal* once described him as "the clown prince of CEOs" and praised his "bellicose good humor." (If you have a dictionary handy, you'll find that it is meant to be a compliment.) As a result, his entire company is infected with a wonderful sense of humor. Employees are famous for making jokes and playing funny pranks on flights, and everyone seems to be having a good time in their work. What a contrast to the workplaces of many of Southwest's customers. Maybe we can learn a few lessons in management by taking a flight on this airline. Anyone want to meet me in Las Vegas next weekend?

Your own feelings are a powerful influence over the feelings of your employees. As a manager and leader you cannot expect your employees to be more positive and energized than you yourself are. Your emotional state and your degree of motivation and enthusiasm are a natural ceiling on what is possible in your employees. That means managing other people's attitudes needs to start with managing your own attitudes.

You can therefore do a very simple exercise as a starting point for managing attitudes and feelings in your workplace. You can check the mirror. Stop and take a good hard look at yourself, focusing on how you feel and how positive or negative you are. Here is an exercise we often use in live workshops that managers say they find helpful.

Exercise 2-1. Checking the mirror.

Please take a moment to answer these questions about your own emotional state in the workplace. Rate each statement from 1 = strongly disagree to 5 = strongly agree. Try to be completely honest with yourself.

Descriptive Statements

How well do these statements describe you?

Strongly Disagree *to* Strongly Agree

I feel enthusiastic about my work most of the time.	1 2 3 4 5
I believe my employees are very skilled and capable.	1 2 3 4 5
I am excited about the possibilities I see at work right now.	1 2 3 4 5
I am usually happy when I'm interacting with my employees.	1 2 3 4 5
I have a lot of energy for my work.	1 2 3 4 5
I believe my current projects are important.	1 2 3 4 5
I am not discouraged by my work.	1 2 3 4 5
I am not tired when at work.	1 2 3 4 5
I am not irritable when at work.	1 2 3 4 5
I am not angry when at work.	1 2 3 4 5

Now please total your answers by adding up each of the numbers you circled:

Total = _____

Interpreting your score:
A score of 10 to 25 is very low. A score of between 26 and 35 is medium low. A score of between 36 to 45 is medium high. A score of 46 and over is very high. As a manager, you will find your employees do not generally have scores higher than your own on this scale. Your score acts as an upper limit on theirs because your mood has a significant influence on theirs.

As we travel through this book together, I will often be asking you to think about your employees' attitudes and how to improve them. Remember however that *your own attitude* has a powerful impact on theirs. It can act as an upper limit, preventing them from being more positive and motivated. Fortunately, the principles of motivation are universal. They apply just as well to managers as to employees, and just as well to ourselves as to others. Many managers find that they end up using some of the techniques they learn for themselves as well as their employees.

In later chapters you'll learn techniques—such as adjusting the level of challenge or rephrasing negative statements—that you can apply as well to yourself as to your employees. *Good self-management is always at the heart of good management.*

The Power of Interpersonal Behavior

As important as your own feelings are, they are only one part of how you influence the feelings of your employees. Your behaviors, how you act around your employees, are also powerful influences. For example, if you ask employees for their opinion before making a decision that affects them, they may feel good about being included. Your effort to invite their participation can make them feel that their role is valuable, and it can increase their interest in their work and in how to do it better. As simple a behavior as asking the right question at the right time can have a big influence on employee behavior.

Take the opposite situation from the one just described. Imagine a manager who makes a decision without consulting employees, then announces it to them. How might this behavior influence the feelings of the employees in question? In general, employees are less likely to feel positive and their motivation usually goes down a bit when they feel like they have been excluded from decisions that affect their working lives. That is in fact what happened in both of the cases we've looked at earlier in this chapter. In the first case, where Juanita is introducing new initiatives in a bookstore, she did not include employees in the development and planning, she just gave them their marching orders. Her ideas were probably excellent, but she made a mistake by not considering how her presenting them might affect the feelings of the employees on whom she must count to implement those ideas.

Also think about the other situation, where you imagined you were working in a depressing location of a big company and your boss assigned you to a new quality team. There too the manager simply assigned a job without thinking about how it should be communicated. As a result, the way in which the assignment was presented made you feel like it was being arbitrarily pushed on you. In both of these cases, you can see that the way in which the manager communicated with employees had a negative impact on their feelings and attitudes instead of boosting motivation.

So *interpersonal behavior*—the ways in which people interact with each other—is an important influence on employee attitudes and feelings. Much of this book is about how you can manage your own interpersonal interactions with employees so as to maximize their motivation and performance instead of damaging it.

In both situations, there is also the problem that underlying attitudes are negative instead of positive. Juanita's employees are most likely looking at their work from a negative perspective. She has probably inherited employees who are on the resistance path and are extrinsically motivated. Same with the second case, where there is a long history of negative workplace attitudes to overcome. In such situations, you cannot expect employees to respond positively to new proposals and initiatives. That ignores the power of their feelings to shape their responses.

To solve the problems in either of these cases, you would have to start by working on building more positive attitudes and feelings. Your first actions would have to be aimed at changing the underlying attitudes of the employees. Once you build good emotional foundations, then you can introduce new initiatives with success. So initially, your interpersonal interactions with employees may need to be focused on building healthy attitudes rather than on specific tasks you want them to perform.

Other Influences You Can Manage

We've looked in the mirror to see how our feelings and our behaviors as managers can influence the feelings and therefore the performances of our employees. Are there any other influences we have control over as a manager?

Come up with any? Let's compare notes. One thing that has a big influence on employee attitudes is the feelings and attitudes of *other employees*. At work, we are surrounded by other people, and often must work with them (or even against them) to accomplish our goals. What if some of these people are negative, unhelpful, uncommunicative, or obstructive? Then they will have a negative impact on our motivation and can even push us onto the resistance path.

As a manager, you need to keep one eye on your own feelings and behaviors and the other on the interactions between your employees. If you see really negative things going on, you need to intervene rather than look the other way. For instance, you want to be proactive in helping your employees resolve any disputes or conflicts they have—not by telling them what to do but by encouraging them to find productive resolutions themselves.

The *physical environment* in which employees work also has

an influence on their feelings and overall level of motivation. Later, we will be looking at aspects of the work environment and their influence on attitudes and performance. As a manager, you can often make subtle changes in the work environment (or better yet, help your employees do so) in order to make sure the influence is positive, not negative. There are in fact a great many ways in which you as a manager can and do influence important feelings and attitudes that in turn shape workplace performances.

The Eyes of the Beholder

It is essential to remember that your employees only respond to their *perception* of your feelings and behaviors, and to their perception of their fellow employees, their work environment, their customers, and any other factors that might influence their type or level of motivation. You may feel really great, but if you close your office door, how will your employees know? You may really like a new program, but if you don't ask them what they think, you can't be sure your employees like it too. People's feelings are shaped by their perceptions of the world around them. All that matters is the eye of the beholder. So it is important to make *sure* you understand how your employees are feeling—and to make sure they understand you too.

Summary

As a manager, you cannot directly influence or control how your people feel about their work. But you have many indirect ways of influencing this important factor. How you feel about work affects how they feel, so managing your own work-related attitudes is a good way to manage theirs. Also, your behavior toward employees can have a big influence on their attitudes. Managers are rarely fully aware of how important their own behavior is. This book will help you learn to manage employee attitudes and behaviors through skillful management of your own behavior.

Herb Kelleher, the CEO of Southwest Airlines, is often asked to explain how his company manages to get airplanes turned around and ready to go out on new flights so quickly (the company does it about twice as fast as most competitors do). According to a *Wall Street Journal* interview with Kelleher, there is nothing to it but a highly motivated group of employees: "We've had people come in to see how we turn around planes. They keep looking for gimmicks, special equipment. It's just a bunch of people knocking themselves out."

Those intangibles at work—and what a difference they make!

CHAPTER 3

Rethinking Management Communications

Employee surveys generally reveal that employees feel they do not have full, open communication with their managers. In addition, poor communications is often a top reason given by employees who have quit a job. If communications are not good, top performers will often seek employment elsewhere.

Restricted communication is a source of frustration and complaints, yet most managers are not fully aware of the importance of this employee concern. Looked at another way, it is also true that when communications are exceptionally open, employees feel more involved and committed to their work and describe their managers as motivational leaders. This chapter will focus on how to use an open, motivational style of communication to build employee motivation and help employees develop rising levels of competence and commitment.

Trouble in the Corner Office

I usually collect business success stories rather than stories of failures, but sometimes it is important to stop and look at what went wrong so as to learn from others' mistakes (instead of making our own!). Here is one such story that really caught my ear because it underscores the importance of attending to communications and using it as a positive management force, rather than just communicating in service of one's latest plans or goals.

A CASE IN POINT

When a director of the San Francisco Museum of Modern Art (SFMOMA) was ousted by his own board of directors, a journalist decided to find out what went wrong. Dale Eastman published his findings in *San Francisco* magazine (January 2002), and his lengthy article included numerous quotes from employees. These quotes provide an interesting perspective on a leadership effort that fell short of employee and organizational needs. The director in question—his name is not important—was a man of vision and energy who raised millions and purchased record quantities of art to boost his museum to the top tier internationally—but he also failed to cover some of the basic leadership bases according to Eastman's postmortem analysis.

More than anything else, his communication style got him in trouble. In particular, his staff found his energy and enthusiasm confusing—they weren't sure what the agenda was at any point in time. And they seemed to lack clear communication from him about what they should be doing and where the museum was going. Here are some of the employee comments gathered by Eastman:

▶ "He didn't say, 'Let's sit down and figure out what we're doing,' so you never quite knew what he wanted."

▶ "He definitely had a temper, and sometimes he acted like a little boy—he'd just have to vent."

▶ "If he didn't deem you to be of primary importance to him, you didn't exist."

These speakers and other employees complained loudly about their leader, contributing to his fall from grace with the board. In general, successful leaders have excellent communications with their constituents, while unsuccessful ones often fall short of this ideal. Like this director who lost his job before he could complete his objectives, many managers seem to have difficulties communicating with their staffs.

What exactly does the leader need to be doing to make employees feel like they are part of a winning team and not just pawns on the leader's chessboard? A lot of this mysterious success (or failure) comes down to the leader's approach to communications. Successful leaders look to their communications with employees as a way not only to get something done—to give instructions, as it were—but to develop the performance potential of those employees and the organization as a whole.

The Principle of Motivational Communication

Motivational communication is any communication that has the goal of stimulating employees' engagement by asking them to get involved in whatever you are thinking about. Engagement means emotional commitment and focus, and it also means intellectual involvement. In fact, high engagement with any task is always a combination of emotional and intellectual involvement.

This engagement or involvement goal is in addition to, or even instead of, the normal goal of communicating the substance of a topic. Traditionally, managers have practiced topic-oriented communication and not focused on the transformational power of the communication itself. The message was functional, not motivational. That is because most manager-employee communications are task-oriented, not people-oriented, as Exhibit 3-1 shows. When you assess managers' communication patterns and leadership styles, you find that they tend to communicate a strong focus on work goals, but very little about any goals for developing the commitment or competence of their people.

Traditionally, when managers did decide to focus on motivation, not just the functional aspects of work, they tended to focus on motivation as if it were something quite independent of normal work that could be quickly turned on to make people work harder. There is a tradition of thinking that if you cheer people on or shout

EXHIBIT 3-1. The average manager's focus. ————————————

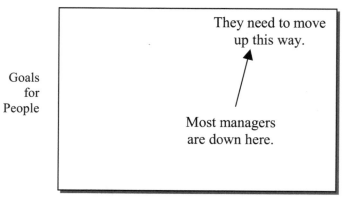

They need to move
up this way.

Goals
for
People

Most managers
are down here.

Goals for Work

---

at them, they will somehow become motivated and work extra hard. But durable intrinsic motivation is not created by cheerleading or shouting at people to work harder—it has to arise from within as a natural response to the circumstances. Motivation needs to emerge naturally in employees as a result of their perception of the work situation.

Motivational communication techniques are powerful tools for stimulating these natural feelings of motivation. They work in subtle ways to tap into the natural enthusiasm and achievement motives of employees who are highly engaged with their work. To understand the distinction between functional and motivational communications, consider the following example.

A FUNCTIONAL APPROACH TO A PROBLEM

For example, imagine that Henry is a shift manager at a distribution center who faces a situation in which 20 percent extra volume combines with several people out sick to create problems on his shift. Henry naturally is concerned with the problem of how to handle the higher volume with the available people. He may decide to shift some people from one role or position to another, to ask some people to do extra work, to postpone the less urgent work, or to solve the problem in some other way.

Then Henry will probably tell the employees on the shift what to do in order to implement the chosen solution. His is a functional approach to communicating because his communications serve the purpose of getting a specific job done—in this case, overcoming the problems to complete the shift's work on time. If Henry has a good solution, and communicates it clearly and politely, the communication will probably serve its intended function well. The problem will be solved.

But there will have been little or no broader benefit because the communication was not designed to boost motivation or build performance potential. Henry had no employee development goal in mind, so the communication was not designed to be motivational or educational in any way. It may have solved the current problem on Henry's shift, but it will have done nothing to keep people from calling in sick in high numbers in the future. And it will have done nothing to prepare Henry's employees to solve such problems on their own. Henry's approach made his people more dependent on him instead of inspiring them to be more competent and self-sufficient.

Stop and think for a minute about alternative approaches Henry could have used. What would you have chosen to do in this same situation?

A Motivational Approach to the Same Problem

If you are facing the same problem that Henry faced, and you want to both solve the problem *and* use it as an opportunity to build employee performance potential, your approach should be quite different. You may still analyze the problem and come up with multiple solutions. But instead of telling employees what to do, give the employees an opportunity to come up with their own solutions. Use motivational communication by, first, explaining the problem to your employees, then, second, stimulating them to come up with possible solutions. Third, facilitate the employees' selection of a solution and, fourth, make sure your employees figure out how to implement their solution well. Finally, oversee your employees' work by providing information or help as needed to ensure success.

In other words, use a participative problem-solving process. Unlike Henry, who just worked out a solution on his own and then told people what to do, use the problem as an opportunity to engage your employees in their work and bring them to a higher level of involvement, interest, and motivation.

The participative approach to problem-solving is illustrated in Exhibit 3-2. It can serve as a reference in case you want to use it later on with a problem at your work.

A Participative Problem-Solving Process

The following process can be used to build employee motivation through their participation in problem-solving—and it also produces high-quality solutions to problems. We'll explore many techniques and skills throughout this book that can be of help in using this process in your workplace.

- ▶ Present the problem (tell them about it)

- ▶ Stimulate problem-solving to generate many alternatives (ask for ideas noncritically)

- ▶ Facilitate selection of best alternative (ask them to evaluate and improve ideas)

- ▶ Facilitate planning of implementation (ask them how to implement the best idea)

- ▶ Supervise implementation (ask them for information about how it is going)

This is the exact sequence of actions described above as an alternative to Henry's approach.

How Motivational Communication Boosts Motivation

A participative approach to the problem in the example above might generate the same solution that Henry would have chosen. Or it

EXHIBIT 3-2. Participative problem-solving process. ───────

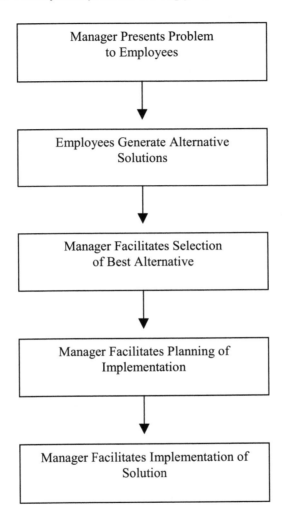

might generate a new solution that is better than any Henry would have thought of without employee input. It *won't* generate a *worse* solution, because Henry will guide the employees toward a solution at least as good as any he has thought of. So the participative approach to the problem does not need to sacrifice quality. It is at least as effective as a more traditional functional approach.

Importantly, the participative approach has an additional benefit because it creates some positive changes in Henry's employees. When their manager involves them in the problem and its solution, they:

▶ Get the message that their job is to take initiative and solve problems, not just do what they are told

▶ Get the message that the manager cares about their ideas and values their abilities

▶ Are able to see the links between what they do and the bigger goals and purpose more clearly

▶ Spend a lot more time thinking about their work, instead of just doing it

▶ Become engaged as creative problem-solvers, not just doers

▶ Learn motivational communications skills themselves because the manager has modeled them effectively

Employee communications designed to achieve motivation-oriented objectives such as these are motivational communications. Communications designed only to get the work done are functional. As a manager, you can tune your ear to this difference. You should be able to classify communications whenever you hear another manager speaking with employees—or when you get a chance to read their e-mails and see their memos or other written communications. And you should also practice listening to *yourself* until you find it easy to tell the difference between communicating with a functional orientation, and using a motivational style by adding employee development objectives.

Col. Len Marella, Ph.D. (U.S. Army retired, now principal of Spring Ridge Financial Group), was quoted as saying, "People want to be a meaningful part of a team and feel that they're contributing." (From *Incentive* magazine, January 2002, p. 14.) I think this is a wonderfully clear and simple insight that sums up the basic rationale for a participative approach to problems such as the imaginary Henry faced in the above case history.

A Leadership Exercise

Joan's manager stops at her workstation and drops a pile of folders on her desk, saying, "This batch just came in late and we need to turn them around by the end of the week. Think you'll have time to get to them?" Joan glances up from her work, says, "Not again!" then sighs and says, "I guess so." Her manager says "Great, thanks," and heads off to talk to another employee.

Question: Is this a functional or a motivational communication?

Answer: The manager did not make any effort to build involvement, engage the employee in the problem, or otherwise encourage participation. The manager simply gave out the assignment. It is a functional communication that will not help build Joan's motivation or stimulate her development as an employee. (What would you have said to Joan if you wanted to take a motivational approach?)

Targeting the Feelings That Influence Actions

Because of its nonfunctional benefits, motivational communication has a direct impact on how people feel about themselves and their work. Functional communications generally target only what people do, not how they feel or what they think. Motivational communications target attitudes, the feelings and thoughts behind employee actions. That is the fundamental difference between functional and motivational approaches to communication.

When Communication Hurts Motivation

You can think of motivational communications as addressing actions indirectly, through the attitudes behind actions. And you can think of functional communications as addressing actions directly while ignoring feelings. But does that mean functional communications do not affect feelings? Just because the manager is not focusing on motivation, does this mean functional communications have no impact on motivation?

No. Functional communications may still affect how people feel, even though feelings aren't the target of functional communications. The museum director described in the opening story of this chapter did not mean to make employees feel frustrated or confused or unimportant, but still, employees report that they had these feelings when working for him.

Many functional communications have accidental or unintended effects on employee feelings. And because these emotional effects are not planned, they are rarely beneficial. Often communications that managers intend to be strictly functional end up having a negative impact on how the recipients feel. The employee may not say anything to indicate that the communication has had a negative impact on motivation, and the manager rarely is aware of this negative impact, but the impact is very real nonetheless.

How Does Joan Feel?

Think back to the example of Joan described above. How do you think Joan felt when her boss put that pile of extra work on her desk? Exercise 3-1 presents some options.

Exercise 3-1. Joan's feelings.

Check the words you think are most likely to express Joan's feelings right now:

1. ❑ Enthusiastic
2. ❑ Frustrated
3. ❑ Eager

4. ❏ Resistant
5. ❏ Excited
6. ❏ Demotivated
7. ❏ Determined
8. ❏ Discouraged

As you may have noticed, the odd numbered choices represent positive feelings and high job motivation. The even choices represent common negative feelings that hurt job motivation and performance. Joan probably felt most or all of these negative feelings (#2, 4, 6, and 8).

When Joan's boss dumped the extra work on her desk, Joan probably felt sad or frustrated or even angry. But the communication, being functional in style, did not address these feelings. As a result, *Joan was left to manage her own feelings about the work.* Her boss's focus as a manager was on the work, not on the attitudes that determine how much work will be done, or how well or willingly it will be done.

What impact did Joan's interaction with her boss have on her job motivation?

Every interaction a manager has with an employee falls into one of the following motivation categories:

▶ Positive impact

▶ No impact

▶ Negative impact

Joan's interaction with her manager in the example above probably had a negative impact on her motivation level. She probably felt discouraged, fed up, or exasperated. We can easily imagine her muttering to herself, "I've had just about as much of this as I can take. Maybe it's time I started looking for another job." And that's not a good frame of mind with which to tackle an extra workload! Yet functional communications, with their single-minded focus on getting the work assigned and done, often do have unintended negative consequences for employee motivation.

Overcoming Barriers to Motivational Communication

The reason motivational communication is essential to motivational management is that *employee motivation is a feeling.* People *feel* motivated, or they don't. If an employee feels unhappy about an assignment, that feeling is in essence negative motivation. Feelings and thoughts combine to shape behaviors, so when you have negative feelings, they are bound to get in the way of great performances, even if the thoughts, the necessary information and knowledge, are present. Joan in the above example will not feel good about doing the extra work the way it was presented to her. Exercise 3-2 presents a better approach to her problem.

Exercise 3-2. A participative problem-solving approach.

One way Joan's manager could have motivated Joan to feel more positive about the extra work would have been to engage her by using the participative problem-solving process. Using your imagination, write down what you might say to Joan for the first two steps in that process:

1. Present the problem:

2. Stimulate problem-solving to generate many alternatives:

Sample Solution

To get the process started you might first say, "I've got a problem, Joan. A batch just came in late, but we still have to turn them around by the end of the week in order to make our targets." Then, you could stimulate Joan to think about ways to solve the problem by saying something like, "Can you think about how to handle this batch and come up with some ideas we can discuss tomorrow morning? There must be some way to get this batch done on time."

When you next ask Joan about it, she is likely to have gotten through her initial negative feelings about the problem and to have come up with one or more productive ideas about what to do. She may actually volunteer to do the extra work—in which case she will certainly tackle it with more enthusiasm and energy than if you had simply assigned it to her!

Summary

Managers need to use communication to boost motivation, not just to focus on getting work done. The manager's role is to get work done through others, not just to do the work. And that means the manager's effectiveness depends on how motivated the employees *feel* about the work. Yet it is a challenge for many managers to take on responsibility for how their employees feel about their work. A good first step to tackling this challenge is to be more aware of the motivational impact of each manager-employee interaction. When you start to consider work-related feelings, not just functional aspects of work, then you enter the realm of motivational communications.

But it often seems difficult to motivate people through your interactions with them. When managers try to be more motivational, they often find themselves struggling to say something inspiring or to articulate highly compelling goals. Sometimes that is appropriate, as we'll see later in this book. But most of the time, motivational communications can be far simpler and easier. You can usually motivate employees without having to stand up on a soap box and waving your arms in the air.

Most of the time, simple communications techniques that build engagement are all you need to use. Something as simple as asking employees to think about a problem and to suggest solutions can be sufficient to get them engaged and to build a high level of motivation. In the next chapter, you will learn motivational communication techniques that are easy to use and require little or no extra effort on your part, yet often have a significant positive impact on employee motivation.

CHAPTER 4

Using Motivational Communication Techniques

Communications is perhaps the most *subtle* art. Two people might say the same words, but one might motivate and inspire employees and the other might turn them off. Generalizing about motivational communications is therefore a dangerous game. If, for instance, I were to simply leave you with a piece of advice such as, "Be sure to ask employees lots of questions," would I be steering you right or wrong? Well, it all depends . . . but on what? In this chapter I want to dig a little deeper by examining some very specific communications techniques and by being clear and specific enough to ensure that what I recommend is highly likely to work.

Is Asking Questions Motivational—or Just Plain Irritating?

How a leader uses questions is an important thing—for questions are very powerful and can be seen as critical or confrontational if not phrased and delivered just right. A good leader certainly tries to ask a lot of questions. But sometimes an interest in the facts and a desire to draw out ideas from others can raise defenses and anger others.

A CASE IN POINT

Lawrence H. Summers took over the presidency of Harvard University in mid-2001, and he immediately began to attract negative publicity and to anger some of the faculty and staff. One highly publicized rift was with Harvard professor William Julius Wilson, who threatened to move to Princeton after an angry meeting with his new boss (and later actually did). Wilson was quoted by *The New York Times* as saying that "his behavior has been quite shocking."

Yet Summers had no intention of shocking anyone and was quick to work on patching up this and other early rifts. What was it that created the widespread impression that this leader was unwilling to listen to his people and difficult to work with? He certainly values listening and wants good communications—he even maintains regular office hours during which anyone can come speak with him without an appointment, a far more generous open-door policy than most executives have. Like many leaders, Summers may have found that his very position of power made it difficult to appear truly open and interested as he interacts with his people.

And paradoxically, it may have been Summers's use of *questions*—a widely prescribed listening tool—that contributed most to his reputation as a poor listener. "If you have a short time with him, it's not too encouraging if the whole time he spends a lot of time challenging your views, even though he may not really believe that," says Trevor Cox, president of Phillips Brooks House, Harvard's umbrella community service group (*The New York Times*, January 6, 2002, p. 18). Summers quickly built a reputation for asking blunt and often alarming—to the listeners at least— questions in meetings. In response, Summers explained, "I think the questioning is a mark of respect for people, an interest in what they have to say. I've always believed you can't do anything without a sense of the pros and cons."

Questioning can, as Lawrence Summers says, be a mark of respect for those you question. But only if you are focusing on *them*— thinking about how to draw out *their* views and sharpen *their* thoughts. In many cases, leaders find their attention drawn to the decision at hand, and so they blast a series of questions that may help them clarify their own thinking. When you are caught up in your own analysis, you can easily ignore the people side of your work—focusing on the "hard" aspects of the decision and possible outcomes to the exclusion of your motivational communications goals.

To avoid the question trap Summers seems to have fallen into, it may be wise to jot down your personal ideas and questions in a notebook as you talk—but not voice them right away. Instead, play the friendly reporter role in the conversation: Simply draw out a detailed, thoughtful presentation from the person you are listening to. Use your questions to probe *their* ideas and feelings, not your own. That is the mark of respectful listening: an obvious, active interest in what the other person's views are, not in developing your own.

Okay, okay—you are in a hurry and you want to make a good decision quickly. And you think your people should be respectful of you as well. Fine! But think about this: Who is more likely to give you an open, fair hearing when it comes time to present your views—someone to whom you have listened with full respect and interest, or those whom you have cross-examined as if they are just there to brief you, the great decision-maker, and then to be led back to their cubicle?

Okay, Now Let's Do it Right!

I don't mean to emphasize the negative here, although there are certainly many ways to make communications demotivating to employees—often quite by accident, as the above case illustrates. However, there are also many ways to transform employee interactions positively using motivational communication, and we will look at some of these positive approaches in the rest of this chapter.

Specifically, we will look at how to make communications motivational by inviting participation and by stimulating thinking. Both of these communications goals boost the employee's involvement and help to make sure they feel committed to the course of action decided upon as a result of the communication. And there are effective techniques for achieving each of these communications goals in a variety of settings and media. The techniques work one-on-one or with small groups and teams, and they can be used in face-to-face communications, or with the telephone, e-mail, written/faxed memo, or videoconferences, or over a Web-cam.

The medium is not nearly as important as the manager's goal

and technique or approach. Each of these general goals is explained and illustrated with concrete examples and techniques in the rest of this chapter.

Invite Participation

Inviting participation means drawing employees out and also drawing them in. You draw them out by signaling that you want to listen to their ideas or concerns. You draw them in by focusing their attention on a specific decision or concern of your own. Any techniques that achieve both of those goals—that get employees to open up to you and get them to focus on an important topic—are going to be motivational. We will look at some specific techniques in a moment, but first let's discuss *who* should be invited to participate.

It is easy to make the mistake of limiting the number of people you invite to participate to only those who you think will have helpful information or knowledge you do not have. That is a functional approach, designed to help you make an executive decision. A motivational approach recognizes that *anyone who might feel they are affected by the topic (the issue or decision) should be invited to participate*. Even people who you do not need to include from a strictly functional point of view must still be included if the topic would seem relevant from *their* point of view.

So the first step is to identify the participants you wish to include. They will typically be people who are likely to have to do the work, to know a lot about the work, or to feel that any changes might affect their work. Then, once you are clear on who to invite into your thinking on the topic at hand, you can apply the following techniques:

- ▶ Asking open-ended questions instead of closed questions

- ▶ Listening more and letting others do more of the speaking

- ▶ Asking lots of questions to find out what others think and encourage them to explore the issue more fully and creatively

▶ Encouraging others to share thoughts through your nonverbal behavior

▶ Stimulating their mental involvement with thought-provoking questions

To do any of these things well takes a bit of special knowledge, so we will discuss each in more detail.

Ask Open Questions

Open questions are any questions that give employees lots of room to come up with their own answer. They are the opposite of closed questions, which guide the employee to one, two, or a few likely answers. So open questions make it likely that you will get an answer of the employee's choosing, while closed questions narrow the answers to those you expect or appear to be asking for.

For instance, any question phrased to require a "yes" or "no" answer is a closed question. If a manager says to an employee, "Your reports were late last week. Will they be on time this week?" the employee is going to say yes or no. (If at all possible, the employee will say yes so as to avoid further negative feedback, even if the employee is not quite sure how to get those reports in on time.)

In this example, the manager probably feels she has had a conversation, but the employee feels that he has been given an instruction or order reminding him of the deadline and criticizing him for missing it. So this closed question did not invite participation from the employee. If you were this manager, how might you rephrase the question to invite participation? Any of the following questions is much more open:

▶ "What were the most important factors causing that report to be late last week?"

▶ "Have you given much thought to how to get reports done more quickly and easily in the future?"

▶ "Do we need to make any changes in our reporting process?"

▶ "I noticed that the report was late last week, but I wasn't sure what effect that had. Is it important to get the reports in on Fridays or is that just an assumption we need to reexamine?"

These sorts of questions, if followed by a friendly interest in listening to the employee's ideas and drawing him out, will open up the communication to a surprising degree. Exhibit 4-1 gives examples of common forms of both open and closed questions.

Often the first thing that pops into a manager's head is a closed question or one that is not as open as it could be. Then the chal-

EXHIBIT 4-1. Open vs. closed questions. ───────────────

A. Examples of Open Questions
Why?
Tell me about . . .
What do you mean by . . .
Can you explain that to me?
What do you think went wrong?
How do you feel about this?
Who should we talk to about this?
Why do we do it that way?
Who is affected by this?
What do you think?
Could you come up with any alternatives we could consider?

B. Examples of Closed Questions
Do you know what you are supposed to do?
When do you think you will be done?
Did you know you messed up another invoice yesterday?
Are you willing to sign onto this team project for next month?
Who is responsible for this problem?

lenge is for the manager to re-form the question into a more open version before saying it. If Joan's manager had thought about what to say before dumping the late batch of reports on her desk (in the example we explored in the previous chapter), the result would probably have been a more open question. But instead, Joan's manager asked her if she could get them done by the end of the week—a classic closed question that Joan would find very hard to say anything other than "yes" to.

The idea is to stop and "think before you speak," as the old saying goes! To make this easier, Exercise 4-1 lets you practice rewriting closed questions in more open form. Take a moment to practice this useful motivational skill.

Exercise 4-1. Transforming closed questions into open questions.

Closed version:	Can you rewrite it here in a more open form?
1. Who is responsible for this error?	1.
2. Can you please be more punctual in the future?	2.
3. Did you know that some of the customers are complaining about you?	3.

Sample Solutions

   1. Do you know why this error occurred? Does this error reflect any underlying flaws in our work process that we should maybe consider improving? Can you take a little time to come up with some ideas about how to prevent errors like this in the future?
   2. I'd like to talk to you about punctuality. Can you tell me how you think it's going and what the main issues are?
   3. Can you help me understand better what's behind these customer complaints? I'd like to talk with you about why these customers are

complaining and how we can prevent these sorts of complaints in
the future. What do you think?

In each of the three cases in Exercise 4-1, the suggested solutions are more open because they invite a more thoughtful, lengthy
response and in fact are likely to lead to a dialog in which insights
and ideas are shared. The original versions are too closed because
they are likely to produce very short responses that close down the
dialog and raise the employee's defenses.

Listen More Than You Speak

Once you've used one or more open questions to invite participation, it is important to continue using motivational communication
methods. Otherwise the communication will revert to functional
lines. One simple and powerful method is to try to speak less than
half the time and listen more than half the time. This is surprisingly
hard to do for anyone in a management position because it goes
against the natural tendency of someone in authority to speak more,
and for someone in a lower position to speak less. So managers
need to make a special effort to listen more in order to achieve a
mix in which the employee does more of the talking.

In studies of manager-employee communications, managers
often say they think they are listening a lot, but the actual record of
their interactions shows that they did much more of the talking.
So it can be hard to be accurate in your self-judgment. It helps to
remember that most people have a natural tendency to dominate
conversations with employees when they are in a supervisory role.
Knowing this bias is likely to affect your ratio of listening to speaking, you can make an effort to correct for it by pausing and reminding yourself to listen more patiently and openly to what employees
say, and to keep asking open questions to draw out their ideas and
contributions.

To illustrate the tendency of managers to think they sound more
open to employee input than they really do, here is a classic quote

from one of the biggest and most successful movie moguls of all time, Samuel Goldwyn, who once said, "I don't want any yes-men around me. I want everyone telling me the truth—even if it costs him his job." Hmm. Somehow I doubt his employees found these words reassuring. Managers who send mixed signals like this are not truly open to input. Their doors may always be open (as the old cliche goes), but employees will rarely enter through those doors.

Remember to Ask Lots of Questions

We reviewed the use of open questions rather than closed ones, a technique that makes questions more inviting of participation. But sometimes managers fail to ask any questions, even closed ones. It is helpful to make an effort to convert statements into questions whenever you can. For instance, imagine you are a manager who is preparing to assign several employees to different roles in a team project. You may have a clear idea of who is best qualified for each role, so the natural thing to do is to simply tell them what you want them to do. Instead, you could ask them what roles *they* think each person should play. That way, you go from a directive communication to a participative communication, thereby initiating an interaction that is likely to build their motivation for performing those roles well.

It is natural to feel some anxiety about losing control over your employees when you switch from telling to asking. In the example above, where you are a manager with a clear idea of who should be assigned which role, you might worry that, by asking them what they think, you will end up feeling you have to go along with their choice, even if it is not as good as yours would have been. To avoid this problem and maintain control over the quality of decisions, don't tell them you are going to let them decide. Simply ask them what they think, and encourage an intelligent discussion of the decision. Share your ideas, insights, or concerns indirectly at first, by asking questions that you think will help them think about the same issues you are thinking about. But also let them raise additional issues—you may be surprised to find that you are learning as much as they are in the conversation.

In the end, a participative discussion of a decision, such as how to assign team roles, will end in one of two ways. Either the employees themselves will come up with suggestions or requests that you feel are good, and you will then be able to go along with their ideas. Or the employees will not propose any good ideas of their own, in which case you do what you would have done originally—you will assign them the roles you think are best. And when you do, you can take a little time to explain your thinking, and let them know that if it doesn't work out to everyone's satisfaction, you will be willing to speak about it again. After all, you might be wrong too, and it might be necessary to reconsider the decision in order to get it just right. Experimentation is the path to the most successful business decisions.

By opening an important decision to employee discussion and using your motivational communication techniques, you get employees involved in the decision. That not only helps build their motivation, but it may also improve the final decision. So there are significant benefits to justify the time it might take for you to stop and engage in an open dialogue with employees.

Pay Attention to the Nonverbal Stuff
We all know that nonverbal aspects of communication are important, but it can be hard to notice and manage our own nonverbal communication. Our body language, our tone on the telephone, our style of address at the beginning of an e-mail, our choice of venue for a communication, and even our selection of the communication medium—all affect the way our message is perceived.

For instance, imagine the following scenarios, each an example of a manager named Georgette asking an open question of an employee:

> ▶ Georgette stops Ralf in the hall when Ralf is carrying a large pile of folders and says, "Do you have any good ideas for how to reduce the conflict in your team?"

▶ Georgette sends all employees on the team an e-mail announcing that the company will not be able to pay bonuses because profits are off, then adds a quick note to the bottom that says, "Send me any ideas you have about how to reduce conflict in the team."

▶ Georgette asks Anna, the team leader, for ideas on how to reduce team conflict. But as Anna begins to speak, Georgette's eyes wander from Anna's face, then Georgette crosses her arms on her chest and begins to tap one foot impatiently.

How open is Georgette's grammatically open question when it is packaged in any of these ways? How open and detailed an answer will Georgette get from Ralf, Anna, and the rest of the team if she keeps asking questions in these ways?

The packaging that a manager chooses can send a powerful conflicting message, making it unlikely employees will actually open up, or it can send a powerful signal of interest and openness, turning even a simple, closed question into an invitation.

For example, Georgette might invite all the employees on Ralf and Anna's team to have lunch in the conference room, and bring in some sandwiches and sodas for them. Once everyone is comfortable and has had some food, Georgette might sit down, lean back, make quick eye contact with the group, then say, "So, is it true there's been a bit too much conflict in the team's meetings lately?" This is grammatically a closed yes-no question, but if Georgette then sits back and waits quietly, inviting responses nonverbally, employees may jump right in and initiate an open discussion of the problem rather than just saying yes or no. The setting and the manager's tone and attitude can provide the invitation, signaling clearly that this is an opportunity to open up and explore a problem.

Stimulate Thinking

Inviting employees to open up and get involved in decisions or problem-solving is motivational in part because it gets them thinking about their work. When people question and explore reasons and options, they find their work more interesting and they often think of better ways to do it. To stimulate their thinking, ask about the root causes of events or problems, and ask them to think of alternative explanations or options. Thought-provoking questions are an important management tool.

For instance, if Paul complains about having too little time and too much work to do, you might ask him why he thinks his workload gets out of control. Listen carefully to his answers, then probe to help him identify controllable causes. Some of the factors are of course things he cannot change, but focusing on these will only lead him to feel helpless. If you ask questions that lead Paul to think about things he *can* control, then you will help him feel empowered to come up with practical solutions.

For example, if Paul says that his workload is too heavy because the company had to downsize, you might agree, but then ask, "Well, given we can't undo the downsizing right now, are there some ways to change your approach to work that would solve the problem?" If he doesn't come up with constructive ideas right away, you could ask additional thought-provoking questions, such as, "For example, is it possible that you could simplify some of your work processes? Are there any steps you can take out of your work?" You might also ask whether he could focus more time on the most important projects and give less time to other things, or whether there are some things that he could delegate or pass on to other departments.

Questions such as these will help Paul break out of accepting a problem and encourage him to think proactively about how to improve the situation. And that gives him a feeling of greater control, which is highly empowering and motivational.

Sometimes it is helpful to ask employees what they think the pros and cons of an option are. This stimulates an analytical approach that gets them highly involved in the topic and often raises useful insights as well. Here are some of the types of questions that get employees thinking harder about their work:

▶ Asking for pros and cons

▶ Asking how to implement

▶ Asking who is best suited to do what

▶ Asking for goals (time, amount, quality, etc.)

All of these techniques encourage employees to think more creatively and critically about their work. The combination of creative idea generation and analytical idea selection is powerful and often helps you as well as the employee to understand work better and to come up with improvements and new approaches. And when you get your employees engaged in not only doing their work, but improving their work methods, then they become highly involved and motivated.

Finding the Time to Communicate Well

Managers who simply make every decision themselves, and then announce the decision to employees, spend very little time communicating with employees. This hurts employee motivation, but it economizes on the manager's time. And some managers are under so much time pressure and have so much work to do that they feel they have to save time whenever and however they can. If you find yourself under intense time pressure in your work, you will feel the same way, and it will be hard for you to make yourself stop and use your motivational communication techniques.

Exercise 4-2. Management time management.

How much "management time" or time to actually manage your people do you have? Use this exercise to find out how much time pressure there is on you. The more pressure, the harder it is for you to devote time to good management communications, and the more important it is for you to use the target and focus methods described after this exercise.

In my work, I find that . . .

__ No __ Yes   I have so much of my own work to do that I can rarely
                 take time to help others with theirs.
__ No __ Yes   I do not have many opportunities to have leisurely con-
                 versations with my direct reports.
__ No __ Yes   I have so many things to think about that I cannot re-
                 call exactly what each of my people is doing.
__ No __ Yes   I get more calls, e-mails, and other messages each
                 day than I can easily handle.
__ No __ Yes   I often feel stressed about my work.
__ No __ Yes   I have to hurry most of the time.

If you checked two or more "yes" answers, then your work puts significant
pressure on you and makes it hard for you to focus on high-quality communications with your employees. In other words, your work conspires against
your goal of being a good manager. You need to manage your management
time well in order to overcome this frustrating and common problem.

The Target-Focus Technique

The solution to this time problem is to *target* the single most important issue or decision you face each day and *focus* on it in your
communication with employees. That way, you only have to put
time and care into one single topic each day. Let the others slide
until you have time to focus on them, or, if you must, simply decide
what to do on your own in a functional way.

This target-focus technique is highly efficient. Most managers
find themselves bouncing from topic to topic hundreds of times a
day. They lack focus, and so are caught up in the whirlwind of
events. Hundreds of e-mails, memos, phone calls, faxes, meetings,
and one-on-one encounters pull them continually from one topic
to the next before they have had a chance to deal with the first topic
fully. That is why they feel they have no time to really get engaged
in serious, open communication with their employees. That is why
they feel they have no time to listen patiently to what their employ-

ees say or to stop and ask their employees how they think or what they feel. By targeting one key topic each day and focusing their motivational communications on it to the exclusion of other topics, managers take control of their time and find it easy and rewarding to use techniques that seemed impossible to fit in without the use of targeting and focusing.

As long as you have targeted the most important decision or question of the day and have focused on it in your employee communications, you will be making a big investment in employee motivation each day. And you will be exploring an important issue far more deeply and fully than most managers do. The target-focus technique is therefore a powerful time management tool as well as a useful motivational communication technique.

This technique, like others covered in this chapter, can do a great deal to generate highly self-motivated employees who are ready to perform at a high level, even when faced with the challenges of today's environment.

Summary

Instead of just giving employees functional instructions and information they need to do their work, managers can communicate in ways that give employees the involvement and understanding needed to be highly motivated to do the work well. The motivational approach to communication affects how employees feel toward their work by taking advantage of routine interactions.

Managers interact with employees frequently and communicate with them often. Each of these interactions is an opportunity for building employee involvement and raising motivation. Sometimes managers feel too rushed and stressed to take the time to invite participation and listen to employee ideas and concerns. If you feel that way, then you can target one specific issue or decision and make it the focus of your motivational communications for an entire day. That will help you manage your time and feel more in control of your work, as well as buying you the time to use motivational communications more fully and effectively.

Although many managers are unaware of it, communications can and often do hurt employee motivation. When you only think about the functional side of what to communicate, you are likely to have a negative impact on the employee's feelings, even if just by accident. In motivational communications, you prevent this undesirable negative impact on employee attitudes.

You can invite participation—a core strategy of motivational communications—by asking questions rather than just telling people what to do. And when you ask questions, it is helpful to make your questions as open as possible. An open question invites a more thoughtful, involved response, and thereby builds employee involvement in the topic.

When communicating with employees, you need to be conscious of the nonverbal aspects. Body language, style, location, choice of medium, timing, and other factors may send a stronger signal than your words. It is important to show that you are open, not just to say you are.

One of the best ways to build employee motivation is to stimulate employees to think about their work. This can be done by asking analytical questions, such as why something happens or what alternatives there are to the current plan. Pro-and-con analysis is also a very helpful option.

CHAPTER 5

Tackling the Feelings
That Drive Performance

Are people more productive when they are enjoying their work? This is no academic issue, it is a fundamental management belief that affects nearly every aspect of an organization and its people. In any workplace, you can either have a positive, fun work climate or not. Which do you think is best for business?

Back in "the good old days" of Intel Corp.'s rapid entrepreneurial growth, this Silicon Valley pioneer embraced the notion that work should be fun and that workers work best when enjoying the work and workplace. In fact, the company's mission statement said specifically that one of its core values was "*to have fun.*"

But then the company got bigger and more serious, and a few years ago the word "fun" was struck from the mission statement. Perhaps this is why it has a reputation today as a pretty serious place—or, as *The Wall Street Journal* put it, "Many people in Silicon Valley think of the chip maker as pretty brusque and businesslike" (January 17, 2002, p. B5). Unfortunately, "businesslike" is generally defined as the *opposite* of fun—maybe we ought to think about that.

In early 2002, the company changed tack again (sort of) at the urging of a group of employees who felt that Intel just wasn't as *fun* anymore. Yielding to this pressure, Craig Barrett, Intel's chief executive, was willing to put fun back into the mission statement, but only if it was made clear that the fun was for a serious purpose. So now it reads that a core value is to "have fun—and win."

This story illustrates the ambiguous relationship we have today with fun at work. Is it important for people to feel up and positive and be enjoying their work, or not? For that matter, do leaders who "shake people up" and "put the fear of God in them" and "rule with an iron fist" get better results than managers who try to make sure people are "in the flow" and "excited about their work" and, dare we say it, "enjoying" their jobs? In this chapter we'll explore the issue of how to create the optimal emotional framework for work.

In Chapter 3 we met Joan, the employee whose boss dumped an extra batch of work on her desk, telling her that a new batch had come in late but still had to be processed by the end of the week. Whatever Joan's exact work might be, getting that extra pile of work thrown at her in such a manner is not going to make her feel very good. But traditionally, managers did not worry too much about how their people felt. Employees had a duty, and were expected to perform it whether they felt good about it or not.

How Feelings Drive Motivation and Performance

In this chapter we are going to explore the links between employee feelings and performance in detail. We are going to look at Joan's feelings about her work in more depth, using a useful tool that examines dozens of possible feelings about work and places them on a grid. This tool will help us dig even deeper into the attitudes driving performance than we did in Chapter 3—revealing the foundational attitudes that need to be managed in order to ensure a high degree of intrinsic motivation. The motivational communications techniques of Chapter 4 continue to apply—but you are going to learn how to recognize and focus on underlying emotional states. And sometimes that requires you as a manager to set your concerns about *your own* work aside and just focus on helping employees get into the right frame of mind to tackle *their* work.

Emotional Intelligence Means . . . What?

What we're really talking about here is the notion that how people feel and react *emotionally* is important to their success and to the achievement of successful organizational performances in the workplace. Daniel Goleman (with his groundbreaking book *Emotional Intelligence* and later writings)[1] has done a great deal to interest managers in this notion that emotions matter at work. One of his key points (at least in my mind) is that, as he puts it, "Good moods enhance the ability to think flexibly and with more complexity, thus making it easier to find solutions to problems." Good moods enhance employees' ability to do many things, especially difficult or challenging things. They also make it more likely employees will volunteer to tackle challenges and help coworkers out, rather than just doing "their" jobs and nothing more.

The importance of an up, positive mood to good work is reflected too in the comment of a manager from the U.S. Army, whom I quoted in my earlier book *Making Horses Drink*. Major General Albert B. Akers believes that "if you are not having fun in your job, there is something wrong."

Is this true? *Should* work be fun? If you ask managers whether they think they should make sure their employees are having fun at work, most of them will equivocate and find it hard to agree completely with this principle. It is antithetical to traditional notions of work in traditional command-and-control organizations. Work should be disciplined and perhaps even hard, and most managers feel uncomfortable saying that work should be fun. Yet if you ask those same managers whether they think employees are going to produce good work when they are unhappy, well, the answer is quite different. Most people readily agree that you need to be enjoying your work in order to produce really good results. If work is an unhappy struggle, the results are not likely to be stellar—this much everyone seems to agree on.

What I think we are seeing out there in the world of work today is a *transitional* set of beliefs. Managers are partially aware of the emotional aspects of good performance, but not quite ready to take the leap to managing the emotional climate for performance. It runs against many of our inherited notions about work. For one thing, it's hard to take on the responsibility of providing emotional leadership if you are used to using functional communications. And it is also challenging for managers to figure out exactly how to monitor the emotional performance environment and recognize when (and when not) to try to intervene. That's why we are devoting a whole chapter to a practical approach to this challenge of providing emotionally intelligent leadership in the workplace.

Let's start by taking another look at the case of Joan and her functionally oriented boss—the one who dumps extra work on her desk and tells her to do it by Friday, then goes away to let Joan deal with the problem on her own.

A CASE IN POINT: HOW DOES JOAN FEEL ABOUT HER WORK?

Joan's company is planning to downsize and lay off 10 percent of its employees, but Joan does not know when this will happen or whether it will affect her position. An earlier layoff several months ago cut one of the people in her department and increased Joan's workload as a result. Her boss does not like to talk about the layoffs and generally stays in his office with his door closed on the days when he is in. Many days, however, he is away on business travel, leaving Joan and her associates on their own. But he does e-mail them regularly to tell them what to do or ask them if they have finished various projects yet. (In other words, his communications are usually functional, not motivational.)

Just yesterday, Joan was trying to clear her desk and get out of the office in time to meet some friends for a late dinner when her boss stopped by, tossed a heavy folder on her desk, and told her it was extra work she had to get done by the end of the week. She feared she wouldn't have time to get to it during working hours, so she brought it home and tried to get started on it after dinner. But it was late and she was tired, and she found herself falling asleep over the file and not making much progress on it.

When she came in this morning she found so many new e-mails and memos awaiting her (even though she came in pretty early) that she did not get a chance to go back to that file again. After lunch—which Joan skipped to try to get caught up—her boss came by and asked her how that extra report was coming and whether she'd have it done by Friday like he asked. She replied with a noncommittal "It's going okay, I guess," and her boss went off and shut himself in his office again. (He'd used a closed-ended question and so was not likely to get a truthful answer from Joan, was he?)

Joan considered turning her attention back to that thick file and trying to get the report started. But she just couldn't get psyched about the project and so she busied herself on less difficult tasks until quitting time. Then she wrestled briefly with herself about whether to stay later and work on it, but realized she was pretty tired. Besides, she noticed her boss had left right at five, and she didn't see why she should stay late if he didn't.

As she was packing up to go, she considered taking the file home again, thinking that she could probably get the report done if she spent a few hours on her home computer. But that also seemed like more trouble than it was worth. She realized she just wasn't feeling very enthusiastic about her work right now. She was worried about what would happen on Friday if she didn't have the report done, but she just didn't feel up to doing it. Maybe she would be the next to get downsized, but the way she was feeling right now she wasn't sure she would mind. She could collect unemployment and look for a new job, and, she reminded herself, there were plenty of jobs out there for someone with her qualifications and experience. Maybe one of them would be preferable to this one.

Evaluating Joan's Work-Related Feelings

Let's take a moment to analyze Joan's feelings about her work. Her feelings are obviously affecting her work and how much extra effort she is able to put into it. In fact, she seems to be losing her job motivation as a result of a number of circumstances. To get a clearer understanding of Joan's situation, use the Work Emotions Grid in Exercise 5-1 to analyze Joan's feelings. To use it, simply read the lists of adjectives in each of the four cells and check any that seem to fit Joan's mood well right now. Once you've done that, read the instructions for analyzing your results.

Exercise 5-1. Work emotions grid.

Positive/Inactive	*Positive/Active*
___ Calm	___ Alert
___ Hopeful	___ Motivated
___ Relaxed	___ Optimistic
___ Happy	___ Enthusiastic
___ Peaceful	___ Helpful
___ Content	___ Focused
___ Sympathetic	___ Creative
___ Open	___ Curious
___ Safe	___ Determined
___ Satisfied	___ Energetic
___ Secure	___ Confident
___ Warm	___ Cooperative
___ Total	___ Total
Negative/Inactive	*Negative/Active*
___ Pessimistic	___ Angry
___ Tired	___ Stressed
___ Sad	___ Resentful
___ Powerless	___ Resistant
___ Uninvolved	___ Defensive
___ Bored	___ Protective
___ Weak	___ Aggressive
___ Uncertain	___ Competitive
___ Fearful	___ Jealous
___ Anxious	___ Restless
___ Unhelpful	___ Pressured
___ Uncooperative	___ Selfish
___ Total	___ Total

To analyze your results from the Work Emotions Grid, simply count the number of checks in each cell. (Each cell has a list of twelve descriptions of feelings, so you can have as many as twelve checks per cell.) One of the cells almost always has significantly more checks than the other three. This high-scoring cell tells you what the dominant emotional orientation is. Look at the label in the top of the cell with the largest total to find out what Joan's dominant emotion is according to your analysis. The options are Positive/Inactive, Positive/Active, Negative/Inactive, or Negative/Active. Which option scored highest for you?

Sample Solution

Joan's emotions are clearly negative, and probably more inactive than active. Did you get Negative/Inactive as an answer?

Getting Specific About "Happy" Workers

The Work Emotions Grid in Exercise 5-1 groups feelings according to two dimensions:

1. Negative versus positive (or bottom versus top)

2. Inactive versus active (or left side versus right side)

The negative/positive dimension has to do with how happy, optimistic, and generally "up" an employee's feelings are. When employees have any of the positive feelings in the two top cells of the grid, they are in a positive frame of mind, which means they are ready and willing to feel good about their work. Positive feelings are very important because they unleash intrinsic motivation and lead employees to want to do a good job. Negative feelings do the opposite. They sap work motivation and can even lead employees to want to do a bad job.

The inactive/active dimension has to do with how much energy and action-orientation employees feel. Obviously people go through regular cycles of activity and inactivity. For instance, you have to sleep periodically—a form of inactivity—in order to have the energy to be active and effective. However, when people feel down about their work, they can and often do fall into a lengthy period of relative inactivity, where it is hard to get enough energy to work and where they feel like they are dragging themselves around.

Alone, none of these four dimensions tells you as much as you need to know about your employees' emotional states. Combined, they tell you a great deal. That is why the Work Emotions Grid looks at the combinations of inactivity/activity and negative/positive feelings. Depression is one of the possible outcomes when inactivity is combined with a negative emotional state, for example (and Joan may be feeling depressed about her work right now, don't you think?).

The Goal: Positive and Active!

Ideally, as a manager you want to maximize the amount of time that your employees spend in the top right quadrant of the Work Emotions Grid. You want your people to be *positive* and *active*, and if they are not, then you know you need to attend to their emotional state before you can expect them to put in great performances. In other words, if your employees' feelings are not dominated by emotional states such as alertness, optimism, enthusiasm, helpfulness, and energy, then you've got a motivation problem you need to address at the level of foundational attitudes.

Employees who are feeling positive and active are ready and eager to do what has to be done. They work quickly and well, they are good at solving problems, they learn fast, and they are in the right frame of mind to be creative when the need arises. It is in this positive/active quadrant where intrinsic motivation is strongest and works best for you as a manager—ensuring that you have "turned on" employees who anticipate what needs to be done and who rush to do it well. Such employees are eager to see what they can accomplish. They are internally motivated to do constructive, helpful things. They don't complain about hard work—they see it as an exciting challenge.

Don't Forget to Let Them Catch Their Breath

Of course, everyone needs to rest on occasion, and as a manager you need to allow and even encourage your people to take the occasional rest. When someone has worked really hard on a project or put in extra effort, see that they take a brief break or do something more relaxing for a little while to provide balance. If you do, you can keep them on the positive top half of the grid—and just let them cycle left and right between the active and inactive cells. If you don't ever let them rest, though, they may grow weary and slip from the positive top half to the negative bottom half of the grid.

Don't worry about employees who are in a positive but inactive frame of mind. Many managers instinctively come down hard on anyone who seems to be inactive. And this can turn their positive mood to a negative one. Instead of coming down on them, give them a challenge to rise up to. Inactive employees who are in positive moods are very easy to shift toward productive activity. All you need to do is show them that they are needed by presenting them with opportunities to do meaningful work and with the resources to do it well.

The Emotional Foundations of Team Effort

It is a well-proven (but little known) finding from the field of psychology that *happy people are helpful people*. When people are feeling up and positive, they are quick to step forward and help others out. Helpfulness is easily predicted based on how happy or generally positive people are feeling. This means that when you have an employee in the positive/inactive cell, where they are feeling generally content and happy, you can count on them to step forward and leap back into action when the need arises. So don't worry about it if your people are sometimes in the positive/inactive cell. It is not hard to move them back over to the positive/active cell. You just need to let them know their help is needed. You just need to get them focused on something important, something they understand is worthwhile. (How? You can use the communication techniques we've covered in Chapter 4, and Chapter 6 will cue up some techniques for challenging employees with good opportunities.)

Watch Out for Negative Emotions!

The negative bottom half of the Work Emotions Grid is more dangerous, and you want to keep a sharp eye out for it as a manager.

That is where Joan is right now, and her negative feelings are going to make it very hard for her to be intrinsically motivated about her work. Her performance is bound to suffer, and she will herself suffer from higher stress and probably from depression or unhappiness as well.

Her negative feelings may be on the inactive side of negative right now, but it is possible that she will become more actively negative if what she sees as bad keeps happening to her. She may end up taking action in the form of quitting and searching for another job. And she certainly will take the most common form of negative employee action: resistance.

Resistance is heel-dragging and general unwillingness to do a good job. It can be passive and hard to see—for instance, Joan might just slow down her pace of work and get fewer reports written. Resistance can also take more active and visible forms—for instance, Joan might send that big file back to her boss with a note saying, "I'm too busy, you'll have to get someone else to do this."

There are also indirect forms of active resistance in many workplaces. These arise when employees feel actively negative, but are afraid to express their negative feelings directly to their managers. They then act out their resistance in any way they can get away with. They may scribble graffiti in the bathroom, or help themselves to things from the supply closet that they can bring home, or be rude to customers. Various studies indicate that employees in U.S. businesses bleed their employers of approximately 5 to 6 percent of sales revenues through what they take from their employers (such as padding expense accounts or taking home merchandise). And if it were possible to measure the additional revenues lost from poor treatment of customers, the total percentage would be far higher.

Although some of these employees may well be criminals who routinely steal when they can get away with it, the vast majority are ordinary, reasonably honest people who don't have any criminal history and don't see themselves as criminals. Then why do they take things from their employers and chase customers away? Because they are stuck in the negative/active cell of the Work Emotions

Grid and feel a need to express these feelings through active resistance. But they also feel unable to act directly in ways that will fix the situation by eliminating the underlying causes of their negative feelings. *They feel powerless to improve the situation in their workplace.*

They probably are afraid to take direct action or simply don't know what they can do. And they probably do not feel comfortable expressing their feelings openly to their supervisors. So they act these feelings out indirectly in a natural effort to achieve an emotional balance. *Their employer has to pay, often literally, for the emotional costs these employees feel.* Their resistance is a natural reaction to the negative feelings they experience, and only the strongest extrinsic motivators will work to keep them performing at a reasonable level.

As a manager, you don't want to have to police negative employees. You don't want to have to worry about resistance and its many forms and effects. What you want is positive employees. And, as much as is practical, actively positive employees. How can you achieve this goal?

The Importance of Recognizing Emotional Frameworks

You can think of your challenge as managing employees to keep them in the top right quadrant of the Work Emotions Grid as much of the time as possible. We will explore techniques for doing so later in the chapter, but first it is important to recognize that you can only manage something if you are aware of it and can observe it clearly. If you don't have a good view of something, how can you control it?

Using Observational Tools

To manage work emotions, you need to make sure you have a good clear view of them. You need to make sure you are aware of how your people are feeling. Can you think of any tools or techniques you might use to do so?

One way of course is to ask people how they are feeling. That is simple and direct, so it is always worth trying. However, recognize that most people do not say exactly how they are feeling when asked. Think about it from your own perspective. If someone says to you, "Hi, how are you?" or "How're you doing?" or "How's everything going?" you probably will just say, "Fine. How about you?" You won't stop and assess your feelings in detail, then say, "Well, as long as you asked, I am feeling a bit frustrated and tired at the moment, and somewhat stressed out, and I hope I'm not coming down with a cold, but at least I am happy that those layoffs they were talking about are not going to happen after all, and . . . , and . . ." If you answered the question fully and honestly, nobody would ever ask you again!

As the idea of emotional intelligence catches on, more and more business leaders are being told to take an active, empathetic interest in the lives and feelings of their employees. The idea seems to be to become extremely interested in every aspect of the employee's life. I think this is a misinterpretation or at least a misapplication of emotional intelligence for two reasons:

1. You don't have to play a role comparable to that of the parent of a young child. You aren't responsible for the employees' entire emotional lives, and you don't want to be; you have plenty to manage already. Your only practical interests have to do with their emotional frame as it affects their work and their ability to perform it well.

2. You have some legal limitations on how much you really want or need to know about the personal life of your employees. In the United States at least, most employment law firms advise managers not to ask about details that might be relevant to the employee's health, for example, for the simple reason that employers aren't supposed to be discriminating on the basis of disabilities. The point is that if you don't know about a disability, then you're a lot less likely to find

yourself defending a claim that you discriminated on the basis of it.

Let's say you read a bunch of books on emotional intelligence and decided to ask lots of empathetic questions—only to have an employee begin to confide details of his treatment for depression to you each morning. Now let's further suppose that this same employee is a consistently poor performer and the company eventually decides to terminate him. Guess what? It wouldn't surprise me at all to learn that he found a lawyer who advised him to claim he was discharged because you didn't want someone you believed suffered from depression in your workplace. Oops. So much for trying to be friendly and empathetic!

It makes sense to keep an eye on employee feelings toward *work*—to make sure they are approaching their work with a positive frame of mind (and an active one at least a majority of the time too). But this is a lot simpler than it might at first seem, since you don't have to "get personal" by asking lots of questions about their lives outside of their work. You can confine your empathy by and large to identifying *work-related emotions* and, should they not be in the quadrant you need them to be, putting a little effort into generating some positive energy in the workplace before bothering to discuss specific tasks.

That is why tools like the Work Emotions Grid are helpful for managers. If you keep a copy of it handy, you can quickly use it to *assess the overall climate or mood* in your group of employees, and probably get a far more accurate and detailed picture than if you asked each of them how they are doing. And you can do this without feeling you have to get into private or personal conversations with them about matters that you'd prefer remain extraneous to the work.

If you were Joan's boss, for example, you might notice that Joan is beginning to drag a bit and doesn't seem as motivated as usual. That is a strong signal that you need to take a few minutes to think about how she is doing. You could talk to her about her work, then fill in a copy of the grid based on your sense of how she is feeling.

Attending to the Nonverbal Messages
When you do an analysis of work emotions, try to focus on the way someone looks and sounds, not on their specific words. Your ability to pick up underlying emotions from nonverbal cues is quite powerful when you trust it. And as we already observed, people will tend to say the socially acceptable thing rather than tell you how they really feel. (They may not even have articulated their feelings to themselves, for that matter.) But when someone is feeling angry and they answer your "How are you?" question with a curt, clipped, "Oh, just fine!" you know that they are angry from their tone and bearing. They don't have to tell you in words. Similarly, when someone is tired, they will say, "Oh, fine I guess" with a sigh, in a way that allows you to tune into their underlying tiredness quite easily. The sigh may be all you need to hear, never mind the words.

So trust your instincts and practice listening between the lines to make sure you are using your natural ability to empathize, or to feel the emotions someone else is feeling. Then capture your findings in the grid or in some similar form of note-taking and see what results you get. That is exactly what you did in Exercise 5-1, when you analyzed Joan's feelings. That exercise is the first step toward fixing Joan's flagging motivation and helping her move into a more positive, productive phase in her work.

Many of the best managers have an instinctive ability to sense when mood needs attention and to come up with the right humorous line, smile, or kind word of thanks for all the effort, in order to reset the emotional tone before talking about the next task.

Using Consideration to Overcome Negative Outlooks

When managers have to deal with employees whose performance is inadequate or deteriorating, what should they say? This situation comes up often in the life of a manager, and it will for you if it hasn't already. It is common to feel some hesitation and to try to avoid a confrontation with the employee. But eventually, managers realize they must take action to try to get the employee back on track. Otherwise, the work will not get done, or, maybe worse, it will get done poorly. Of course, the remedy must vary depending upon the cause of the employee's poor performance, but let's look at a fairly common scenario to start with and see how you would handle it.

A CASE IN POINT: WHAT TO SAY TO AN UNDERPERFORMING EMPLOYEE

Imagine you manage a busy group of employees who have a number of important reports to get out by the end of the week. Most of your people are hard at work and on top of what they need to be. But one of them seems to be falling increasingly behind. Each time you asked her about the status of her work she has given you a vague response, never actually admitting that she has a problem but nonetheless leaving you increasingly sure she is not on schedule. You have reminded her several times about the Friday deadline, but now, on Thursday afternoon, you discover that she has not even *started* one of the key reports. What will you say to her? How do you plan to handle this situation?

This case gives insufficient information for a full solution, but it also invites the most common (but usually ineffective) management response to poor performance: To confront the employee with a firm reminder of what needs to be done, perhaps backed up with a hint of the negative consequences if she fails to do so. Is that what your instinct was? It is probably how other managers have handled such situations in your experience, so it is not surprising if you thought of using the same approach. But recognize that this employee has a perspective on the situation that is probably very different from yours as a manager.

This employee has, first of all, an *emotional perspective* that drives her performance. And until you know whether it is negative or positive, you don't want to pressure her about the work. So the best action you can take is to assess her work emotions. If the employee is feeling positive, but just stuck for some reason, then you can focus on the problems with her work and try to come up with a solution to move her forward. But if she is feeling negative, then you need to fix that attitude problem first, *before* you focus on trying to get her caught up in her work.

Did you notice anything familiar about the employee in the case above? She is behind in her work and has not begun a report that her manager assigned her. The manager is naturally going to feel anxious about the work and will tend to escalate the pressure to perform. In other words, this is an employee whose manager keeps using functional communications and has not yet done a proper assessment of her work emotions.

Sounds a lot like Joan from the earlier examples, doesn't it? And fortunately, you have already performed a careful analysis of how Joan is feeling, using the Work Emotions Grid. So you know that Joan's perspective is different from the somewhat narrow perspective offered in the description given above. This description is probably how Joan's manager sees her performance, but not how Joan experiences it.

Joan feels like she is being overwhelmed with work, and she finds her workplace increasingly stressful and unpleasant. She probably feels like her manager is treating her unfairly and overloading her with work. Joan's perspective has made her attitude toward work be dominated by negative feelings, as you saw in your earlier analysis of her emotional state.

But in all likelihood, her manager does not know this. Her manager probably thinks that Joan is a difficult employee. He is likely to blame Joan for her poor performance. And although in the long run we should hold employees responsible for their performance, blaming them for their problems blinds us as managers to the ways in which we can solve those problems. Joan's manager needs to take some steps to try to swing Joan's attitudes up and into the positive range. Otherwise, Joan's work is going to continue to slip.

Manager of Office Football Pool Arrested

Office fun is great for morale—but let's make sure it's strictly legal. A New Jersey office of AT&T enjoyed participating in the football betting pool organized by one of its middle managers. But because the manager kept a 10 percent cut, prosecutors charged him with promoting gambling and are planning to bring him to court. Oops! Didn't mean to have *that* much fun at the office. (Based on an Associated Press report, January 11, 2002.)

Stimulating Positive Feelings

How can Joan's manager shift Joan up into a more positive attitude toward her work, especially now that Joan is having to cope with added stresses and extra demands? We are going to explore this question in many ways throughout this book, but the basic answer is a simple one. There are two things you as a manager can do to help employees maintain positive attitudes toward work:

1. You can make an effort to manage your own attitudes, so that when you interact with your employees you feel up and positive. Your emotions naturally tend to rub off on the people around you, so this is an important first step. So avoid the temptation to go directly to your employees and share your own concerns—when you are likely to be feeling negative yourself. Take some time to recharge and regain your enthusiasm and hopefulness. (Listen to inspirational music, read your favorite book of cartoons, take a walk, review some of your successes, or watch a movie that inspires you—do something you know will reset your mood before you try to reset someone else's.) You will then tend to see the situation in a more positive light, and you will also be more aware of your employees' strengths (rather than weaknesses), so it will be easy to project a positive, enthusiastic mood.

2. You can provide reassurance, support, and consideration. In other words, you can focus on how your employees are feeling and do and say things that are likely to make them feel better. Or even if you don't do anything directly to improve their situation, you can simply let them know you know and care how they are feeling. This consideration will tend to improve their moods. Basically, almost anything you say or do that focuses on how they feel about their work, rather than what they do, will help move them in a positive direction. (And you can always try any of the motivational communication techniques you learned in Chapters 3 and 4, especially those that focus predominantly on feelings rather than tasks.)

When it is necessary to shift one or more employees from a negative to a positive perspective, you can visualize your management role as tipping the emotional balance the other way. Exhibit 2-1 in Chapter 2 showed how employees can react to the same stimulus in two different ways, depending upon their emotional state.

The negative state leads them to the resistance path, and leads you as their manager to an increasingly frustrating reliance on extrinsic motivators. But the positive state leads them to see the stimulus as an opportunity instead of a problem. And so they move up the motivation path, engaging their intrinsic motivation and enjoying the opportunity to perform well at something worth doing. What you are trying to do when you manage your own emotions and when you behave considerately and supportively is to bring about that subtle but vital mood shift before you try to motivate them to do a specific task. Exhibit 5-1 shows this management action as the stimulus, and describes the change in the employee's emotional state that results.

After you have provided appropriate emotional stimuli and helped the employee feel more positive, you can then safely introduce other stimuli that are more task-focused. In other words, you

EXHIBIT 5-1. Managing for positive emotional states. ——————

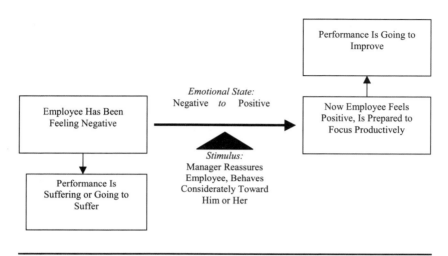

can then safely ask the employee how to get something done or ask him to suggest ways of solving some problem.

Creating an Action Orientation

The shift from negative to positive attitudes is a vital one, but obviously it is not the whole story. It just sets the stage for some serious work. It isn't the work itself. Nobody ever made a dime just from feeling good. You have to convert those good feelings into useful actions to make them percolate down to the bottom line.

The need to follow positive feelings with positive actions explains why the Work Emotions Grid has an action dimension. As a manager, you need to first take care of any negative feelings by creating a positive work atmosphere—and then you need to capitalize on this atmosphere by focusing your people on productive activities. If people are in a positive frame of mind, they are often capable of handling assignments even if those assignments are not managed particularly well. But our goal is of course for you to manage employee assignments well—better than most managers.

The advantage of managing your employees' work especially well is that it keeps them from slipping back to negative attitudes again and it keeps them in an action orientation most of the time. You can do this by making sure that:

- ▶ *Clear assignments*. Everyone knows what they are expected to do.

- ▶ *Sufficient resources*. They know how to do it and have the resources they need to do it well.

- ▶ *Achievable challenges*. Nobody has excessively easy or excessively difficult work, since either extreme is demotivating.

- ▶ *Rich feedback*. They can track how they are doing with clear scoreboards and feedback from as many sources as possible.

- ▶ *Meaningful purpose*. They see why their work is important and what goals it helps achieve.

Don't worry if this seems like a big list for you to manage. We go into detail about how to do each of these things in the rest of the book. You will be getting helpful tools and techniques as well as confidence-building practice exercises to do. But for now, take a moment to at least understand in principle the importance of focusing people by giving them appropriate challenges that have all five of the above characteristics. When you do, you maximize their action orientation and minimize the chances of their slipping back to a negative attitude toward their work. This process is illustrated in Exhibit 5-2, which summarizes the approach you can use to set the stage for high motivation and star performances.

Summary

Employees' work emotions are the attitudes that shape their approach to their work, and there is little point in trying to get employees to do anything unless their underlying attitudes are right.

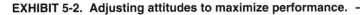

EXHIBIT 5-2. Adjusting attitudes to maximize performance.

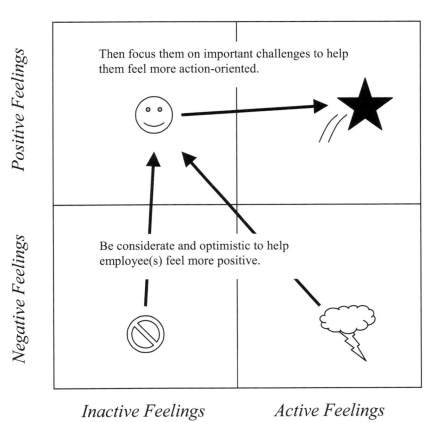

Start by assessing how positive (versus negative) and how action-oriented (versus inactive) your employees are. Being aware of these two dimensions of workplace attitude is an essential step toward managing for high intrinsic motivation and good performances.

Intrinsic motivation and peak performances are associated with a positive, active emotional outlook. If that is lacking, you need to work on moving employees to a more positive frame of mind. Then you need to inspire them to appropriate action by giving them clearly defined, meaningful work that they will feel good about accomplishing—and making sure they have enough feedback to be able to see their progress as they work. The next two chapters will look at how best to use goals and feedback about performance toward those goals as you continue to build the momentum of your workforce.

Notes

1. Daniel Goleman, *Emotional Intelligence* (New York: Bantam Books, 1995).

CHAPTER 6

Providing Challenging Opportunities

> In the long run, people hit only
> what they aim at. Therefore, though
> they should fail immediately, they
> had better aim at something high.
>
> —Henry David Thoreau

I s Thoreau giving good advice? An aspirational goal—something exciting and maybe even a bit scary to aim at—can be highly motivating, giving meaning and purpose to otherwise dull tasks. On the other hand, that bit about "failing immediately" is somewhat alarming. Thoreau may have had more tolerance for failure than many employees do today. If you as a manager set employees up for failure with seemingly impossible goals, you will accidentally hurt motivation instead of helping it. So either way, goals have a big impact on motivation, and they are something you want to use often and wisely as you pursue superior performance.

Goals are essential to every aspect of management because they provide the basic structure for employees' work. I was thinking about this point recently when reading the results of a study by the Incentive Marketing Association, which concluded that employee incentive programs must have three elements to work well:

1. *A clear goal* (make it fair, simple, easy to explain). Nobody participates if they are confused or uncertain about the goal and ground rules.

2. *An incentive with emotional value to participants.* Choose something that employees care about, and help give it additional meaning in the way you design and present the program.

3. *An attainable incentive.* "Expectation of achievement is an integral part of the program's success," according to the association's guidelines in their report, *The Art of Motivation*. Make sure that every participant can *attain* the goal.

In other words: A *clear goal* with *emotional value* that employees see as *attainable*. This is good advice if you want to put together an incentive program to draw attention to a particular goal or challenge. But notice that it is really a great deal more than that. If you look past the specific context of this advice from the Incentive Marketing Association, the advice is pretty good as a general guideline for how to motivate employees to do anything you need done. Basically, they are talking about clear goals (recommendation #1), some level of emotional involvement since nobody pursues a goal they don't care about (recommendation #2), and goals that employees feel are realistic—that they *can* attain, or else why bother (recommendation #3). That's pretty good advice for managing employee performance, whether you choose to attach a tangible incentive to the goal or not.

The Motivational Power of Opportunity

Did you know that opportunities create energy? In study after study, people who are pursuing an exciting goal and are hopeful of achieving it experience high motivation and achieve superior levels of performance. In contrast, dull, meaningless work is exhausting—even (or perhaps especially) when it's easy.

This is true of people everywhere, from the classroom to the board room to the playing fields. Ever notice how young children won't walk a quarter of a mile in a straight line, but will gladly run many miles in play? And studies of athletes show that those who are focused on developing their skills and pursuing personal performance goals not only do better, but have more energy. A recent *Psychology Today* article puts it like this: "They draw on the energy generated by their own goals and aspirations."

That is why Frederick Herzberg, a pioneering researcher who developed the concept of job enrichment, says, "If you want people motivated to do a good job, give them a good job to do." It is a profoundly simple idea, an idea with great power, but sometimes a difficult idea to implement. Managers often feel like they have relatively little control over the work they assign their people, and that it is up to the people to adjust to the work, not the other way around. As a result of this widespread view, most employees do not have the optimal level of challenge in their work. Most people are not doing something that is inherently highly motivating.

Bob Nelson, author of the best-seller *1001 Ways to Reward Employees*, sums up the problem when he says, "Unfortunately, in reality, most jobs are not intrinsically very motivating." But as a manager you have the power to fix this problem.

Just How Important Are Opportunities?
Opportunities are situations in which an employee feels there is a possibility to achieve something significant through good hard work. So opportunities are all about achievement. Give someone a chance to achieve something significant and you are giving them good opportunities that inspire intrinsic motivation. But give them nothing more than a job that must be done to collect their paycheck and you do not appeal to their intrinsic desire to achieve. At best, you appeal to their sense of duty, which may be strong but is unlikely to be anywhere near as sustained and powerful as their desire to achieve.

Everyone has a need for achievement to some degree, making this about as near to a universal motivator as you are likely to find. That is why when employees are surveyed to find out what sorts of things motivate them in their work, opportunities for achievement generally comes at the very top of the list. We will see details of that list of work motives in Chapter 10, when we take a look at individual variation in motives and how to adjust for it.

On average, employees strongly agree with survey statements having to do with opportunities to achieve and feel that this factor is especially important to them in their work. Of course, averages do not express everyone's view, so it is also notable that just about everyone finds opportunity to be an important motivator. In a study of work motives done by my firm, although some people ranked achievement higher than others, almost everyone ranked it at the top of the scale, in the strongly agree to very strongly agree range.

Exhibit 6-1 shows the results from a sample of employees, and in it you can see that bars representing people's scores are clustered at the top of the scale, well above the line that divides the disagree or negative answers from the agree or positive ones. So it is safe to say that almost all employees respond favorably to opportunities and are eager to reap the rewards of achievement.

The "Lever" Motivator

In fact, if you could use only one of the many motivational methods in this book, opportunity would be the one to choose. Opportunity is like a giant lever that can lift attitudes and performance throughout your group of employees and make up for a lack of other motivators. That is why it is essential for you as a manager to *make sure that every one of your people has appropriate, appealing challenges at all times*!

The Difference Between Responsibilities and Challenges

The following exercise explores the appeal of challenges and uncovers some examples that may help you learn how to provide good challenges for your people. The exercise involves examining your own work experience.

Exercise 6-1. Identifying your most recent challenges.

Step 1

Take a moment to think about your own work experience over the last few months. Recall what you were doing and what specific duties and assign-

EXHIBIT 6-1. The importance of opportunities for achievement.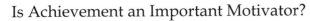

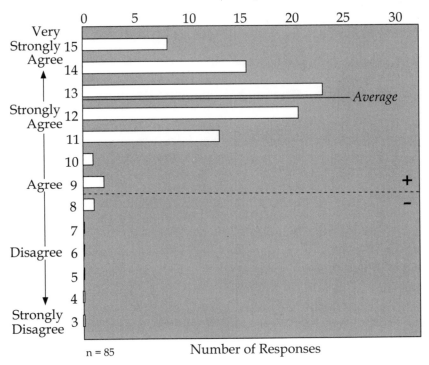

Is Achievement an Important Motivator?

n = 85   Number of Responses

ments you handled. Then write a list of the main duties you were responsible for. (For example, someone who was a buyer for a retail store might list placing orders, checking inventories, meeting with salespeople, and negotiating terms of purchase. Or, for another example, someone who was an office manager might list handling the telephones, filing, hiring new data entry clerks, and preparing monthly reports.)

What main duties were *you* responsible for in recent months? List them one to a line in the box. Ignore the 1 through 5 scales on each line for now.

Your main work duties:

	1	2	3	4	5
	1	2	3	4	5
	1	2	3	4	5
	1	2	3	4	5
	1	2	3	4	5
	1	2	3	4	5
	1	2	3	4	5
	1	2	3	4	5
	1	2	3	4	5
	1	2	3	4	5

Okay, that's step one of the activity. By now you should have a fairly lengthy list of your main responsibilities—the things you would get in trouble for if you failed to do them or messed them up.

Step 2

Now take a look at your list from a different perspective. Go back over it, asking yourself which (if any) of these responsibilities or duties felt like an exciting challenge, one you were eager to test yourself against. Use the 1 through 5 scale on the right hand side to say how exciting an opportunity each one is. Specifically, decide to what degree you disagree or agree with the following description of each of the duties in your list:

"This was an exciting opportunity for me to achieve important, satisfying results."

Strongly disagree = 1
Disagree = 2
In the middle = 3
Agree = 4
Strongly agree = 5

Look over your list and scales in Exercise 6-1 and see how many of your duties also qualified as exciting opportunities for you to achieve important, satisfying results. Did you give any "5" ratings? How about "4" ratings? Fours and fives are associated with truly motivating opportunities, things that make it fun to get up early and rush into work to see what you can accomplish toward your goal today.

I have a strong hunch that you did not circle very many fours and fives (although I hope for your sake you did!). I also have a hunch that you circled some lower numbers, indicating that at least some of your responsibilities did *not* feel like exciting opportunities to achieve. The truth is, most people do not find their duties to be especially exciting. Their responsibilities do not feel like opportunities. But some responsibilities are more exciting than others. Some rise to the level of motivating opportunities. What is the difference between those and the others?

Exercise 6-2. What makes it a motivating opportunity to succeed?

Take a minute to think about the difference between what you did that seemed like exciting opportunities, versus what you had to do but what did *not* appeal to you as opportunities to achieve something important. What were the differences? In general, *what is it that makes an assignment an exciting opportunity to achieve?* Try to come up with three or more factors that make an assignment into an opportunity to achieve something personally important:

> 1.
>
> 2.
>
> 3.

There are a variety of possible answers to the question posed in Exercise 6-2. However, in many cases, the following three characteristics turn out to be especially important:

1. *Purpose*. It's important, it has meaning, it contributes to important goals or needs.

2. *Interest*. It is something that engages your interests and strengths, something you find personally challenging, meaningful, and fulfilling.

3. *Ability*. It is something you are capable of doing (you have the information, skills, and resources necessary to make it possible).

One reason for mentioning the Incentive Marketing Association study earlier in this chapter is that it contained the same three core elements as my firm uses in the design of meaningful opportunities. Remember what the ingredients for a successful incentive program were? It had to have a clear goal with emotional value that you see as attainable, which is virtually the same as saying opportunities should have purpose, interest, and attainability to be motivating.

So, for example, imagine what tasks might motivate Joan, our overburdened employee from the earlier chapters. Remember, she's the one whose boss dumped extra work on her desk and told her to get the report out by the end of the week? We explored the importance of a positive, active attitude for her when we last met her and her dilemma. But now we are talking about the work itself, rather than the employee. Joan's boss had not been in the habit of using motivational communications, and had not realized that Joan's attitude was deteriorating.

Let's assume Joan's boss has learned how to interact with Joan in a more motivational manner, and has put a little effort into reviving Joan's attitude by reassuring her and showing some empathy for her situation. Now, he still has the problem that he has to assign lots of work to his downsized group of employees. So which sorts of assignments should he give Joan if he wants to cash in on the power of motivational opportunities?

Well, he obviously should give Joan assignments that she will see as having purpose and interest, and for which she has the ability to succeed. Purpose, interest, and ability are the three general characteristics that transform an ordinary task into a motivational opportunity to succeed.

But if you were Joan's manager, would that tell you all you need to know to make sure you matched Joan with good opportunities that align best with her sense of purpose, her needs, and her abilities? I doubt it. So far, we really know very little about Joan, aside from what we have learned about her attitude toward work. We don't know what turns her on. We don't know what her aspirations are, which would tell us something about the projects she would be likely to find interesting. (For instance, if Joan wants to move up to a management role eventually, then she might be interested in any projects that gave her relevant experience.)

We also don't know anything about Joan's ability to do any specific task or assignment. (For instance, maybe she has the necessary skills but does not get cooperation from the accounting department and so can't get all the numbers to produce that report we need by the end of the week.) In short, we don't know enough to guess whether Joan is going to see any specific task as an exciting opportunity to achieve—or a dull waste of time, or even perhaps an impossibly difficult hassle.

So how can we tell which sorts of assignments are going to turn Joan on and which ones will turn her off? Or, to put it another way, how can we best structure the work that needs doing so as to make it as appealing as possible?

Finding Out Which Opportunities They Want

The simplest way to find out what Joan, or any employee, thinks is an exciting opportunity to succeed is to *ask*.

Joan knows what turns her on. If asked to choose between two tasks, for example, she would be able to tell you which one seems like the better opportunity for her based on her interests and career goals. Also, she would be able to tell you if there are any reasons why a particular job does not meet the criteria necessary to make it a motivational opportunity. So you could even ask her more specific questions, like . . . hold on, isn't this another fabulous learning opportunity? If you come up with examples of questions that probe Joan's purpose, interest, and ability issues, then you will be perfecting *your* ability to harness the power of opportunities.

Exercise 6-3. Asking questions to explore the opportunity landscape.

Okay, so you want to find out whether an employee sees a project, task, or duty as a motivational opportunity. Or not. And the best person to tell you is the employee herself. So what kinds of questions are you going to ask? Now, if she happens to be an expert on employee motivation, she might be able to tell you how to do your job, so you could just ask her something like, "What do I need to do to make sure you view this job as full of opportunities to achieve?" And maybe that question would generate some good answers even if she isn't an expert . . . it's a pretty good thought-provoker anyway.

But to be sure you get what you need, better also ask some more specific questions. Better probe for insights about purpose, interest, and ability issues. So in this exercise, come up with at least three good questions that you could ask Joan if you were her boss—or that you could use with any employee to help you understand their perspective on opportunity:

1. Question(s) to find out whether the assignment or task seems purposeful:

---

2. Question(s) to find out whether the assignment or task seems interesting:

3. Question(s) to find out whether the assignment or task seems doable:

Sample Solutions

Any questions are good when they give you more insight into whether something seems like an opportunity for achievement and why. Here are some examples of questions that will help:

1. Does this job seem meaningful or important to you? Why/Why not? What is its purpose?
2. Does this assignment seem interesting to you? Why/Why not? How could it be made to include things you like to do and that appeal to you as personal challenges?
3. Do you have the ability to do this well? Are there any things you are missing? Do you have any questions about it?

Identifying Problem Assignments

Let's say that Joan's boss asked her questions about the report-writing work she does and learned that:

1. *The work does not seem important.* Joan thinks it has little purpose, because as far as she knows the reports are just forwarded to headquarters and filed somewhere. If anybody reads them and makes important decisions based on them, she is unaware of it. This job fails the purpose test.

2. *The work does not interest her.* At first, she found it something of a challenge, but she has written so many reports in the last couple of years that each one blends into the next and she can do them in her sleep by now. The work was an

interesting challenge at first, but once she mastered it she no longer found it very engaging. Now she just views it as a tedious chore and takes little pride in it. It fails the interest test.

3. *The work is generally fairly easy to do*. She has more than enough skill to do it, but often there are key pieces of information needed for a report that have to come from another department. When other departments aren't cooperative, she feels some stress because she has no control over the situation. She often gets blamed for late reports when she has been waiting for other departments to forward the needed information, and they refuse even to return her calls and e-mails. Because of this problem, report-writing often fails the ability test too.

In short, Joan is expected to crank out report after report—and even to handle more of them than she used to since the downsizing in her department. Yet the task does not pass the opportunity test. *It does not appeal to her as an opportunity to achieve.*

There is little about the work that makes it inherently motivating for Joan to do. So even if Joan approaches the work with a positive, action-oriented attitude, eventually this work is going to wear her down. Nobody can maintain peak levels of motivation (or performance) when faced with a job like Joan's report-writing assignment. Joan's manager needs to work on this issue right away.

Turning Everyday Tasks into Opportunities for Growth and Development

The first thing that comes to mind when you realize employees do not have motivational opportunities to succeed is to give them something new and exciting to do. That is a great idea and sometimes it is just the thing. For instance, maybe Joan would get really excited about an opportunity to put together a cross-department team with the mission of streamlining the report-writing process. This would allow her to apply her knowledge and experience to making the process better and eliminating the problems she has with lack of cooperation from other departments. She might also be able to come up with some ways to make the report-writing go more quickly so that the downsized department could handle its work-load better and more easily. But—and this is a big but—you cannot always give employees new exciting tasks just because their current responsibilities don't motivate them sufficiently.

Often, at least in the short term, you have to face the fact that there is routine work to get done and somebody simply has to do it. In that case, you need to work on improving your presentation and design of the task. You need to work on redefining the task and the approach to it so that it provides a better opportunity for the employee to feel good about his or her achievements.

The Quest for Challenge

I was recently invited to join a management meeting at a successful company that made special cables for wiring buildings. The managers had read about motivating with opportunities in one of my earlier books, but they had a problem with implementing this idea. They felt it did not apply to their factory, since the work was, in their view, repetitive and highly structured and did not offer much room for employees to pursue new challenges. At the end of the day, each order had to be filled meticulously and carefully, and the employees simply had to put their noses to the proverbial grindstone and do the work. What role could opportunity possibly play? *What* opportunity?

I don't know about you, but I like a good challenge, and this sounded like one to me. So I disagreed, arguing (in spite of my lack of knowledge of the specifics) that there had to be challenges and opportunities for growth in the industry itself, in which case all we had to do was find ways to translate those into some challenging opportunities for employees. The managers in this meeting soon generated a list of the sorts of things the company needed to do to continue to be a success, such as reducing turnaround time on orders, reducing waste material, continuing to improve quality, and making sure there was good clear communication with the customers so that they ordered the right things in the first place.

This simple exercise generated a broad strategic agenda. Next I asked the managers to translate this agenda into some narrower specifics that employees at the production plant might be able to relate to. Could they shave a day off of order turnaround, for instance? Hmm, maybe, but it wasn't immediately clear how. So that suggested the need to come up with some ideas and plans for how to tackle reducing turnaround time. Could employees be challenged to generate some proposals? Sure, why not? If they are currently bored with their work and viewing it as a repetitive routine, then a challenge like this one is absolutely essential to maintaining high motivation, let alone to maintaining strategic momentum in the marketplace.

What I learned from this experience is that there is really no such thing as a job or workplace where opportunity cannot (and should not) be used to motivate. And if you ever come across a situation where there seem to be no meaningful opportunities for challenge and growth, then your first job as a leader is definitely to generate some opportunities!

Using Task Redesign

A good way to increase the achievement opportunities presented by any specific task is to go through a task planning process with the employee. (Task, by the way, refers to any specific, clearly defined assignment or duty. You need to break down overall jobs into the more specific tasks that make them up, since employees experience their work as a series of tasks to be done.)

Exhibit 6-2 is a worksheet you can use for this planning process. It is best to find a time to sit down with this form together with the employee and go through it jointly. You can fill in the blanks if

EXHIBIT 6-2. Motivational task plan form. ——————————————

WHAT? Define the task in terms of *specific* actions and results.
a. *Actions to take:*

b. *Results to produce:*

WHY? Relate the task to important goal(s), objectives, or aspirations.
a. *Importance to organization:*

b. *Importance to employee:*

HOW? Record key skills and resources needed to perform the task well.
a. *Employee performance requirements:*

b. *External resources and support requirements:*

ISSUES? Both manager and employee need to note any concerns or remaining issues here, to keep them on the agenda for possible resolution in the future. (No task assignment is perfect—so make sure you know what the potential problem areas are!)
Manager's remaining concerns, if any:

Employee's remaining concerns, if any:

——————————————————————————————————————

you wish—but try to do it in a cooperative style sitting next to the employee or passing it back and forth so that he has a good view and feels like he is an *active contributor*. You might even try having him do the filling in if you prefer, to make sure that he is fully engaged in the planning process. That is the ultimate in participative planning and goal-setting.

If you do let the employee handle filling in the Motivational Task Plan Form (Exhibit 6-2), have multiple blank copies at hand and don't feel bad about treating it as a work in progress. Keep discussing and improving the plan until you have a version of it you both like. No need to sacrifice anything on the performance side just because you are asking for employee involvement. Don't feel bad about being clear and assertive on what has to be done, how well, and what results you need. As the manager, you are responsible for making sure the work is done and done well, so the employee will understand your need to stick up for good results. This is not an opportunity for the employee to negotiate to do less work. It is instead an opportunity for the employee to advocate for and explore ways of making the work more important and interesting and doable.

Define the Task *Very* Well

In defining what the task or assignment is, you will see that the planning form asks you not only to define the actions the employee must take, but the results the employee should produce. That helps to make the definition of the task especially clear in the employee's mind. And it gives you and the employee ways to check on the task later on. For example, imagine that you are defining Joan's report-writing task, as follows:

A. *Actions to take*: Pull together weekly information on each contract and write up a report summarizing the progress of the work and any problems or deviations from the original plan.

B. *Results to produce*: Produce a neatly printed, accurate report using the template format and submit copies to me and to headquarters each Friday.

The description of what she should produce in "B" makes it clear how to monitor the quality of her work. The report needs to be neat, accurate, in the correct format, submitted to the right people, and submitted on time. These five criteria express everything important about the work. If Joan accomplishes these five goals, she has succeeded. That makes the nature of the task crystal clear. (Or it should. Just make sure you and Joan agree about how to evaluate or measure each criterion. If you find errors she is unaware of, then you need to spend some time going over what you mean and getting more specific about what errors to avoid.)

Make the Purpose Clear and Compelling

Next, the Motivational Task Plan Form in Exhibit 6-2 asks you and your employee to define the things that make this task important—both to the organization and to the employee. In defining the organizational importance, think about what key goal or mission the task helps accomplish. Make sure you and the employee have a clear line of sight from the specific duties and results to the big-picture purpose of the work. This may at first be difficult for you and the employee to do. Too often, the importance of work is assumed, rather than thought through. But unless the employee can see precisely why the work needs to be done, it won't seem important enough to inspire intrinsic motivation.

It is also helpful to explore the employee's aspirations and goals and see how the task relates to them. When employees feel that doing a good job on this particular task is going to provide good experience, help them feel like the work matters, help the company perform well so they can get their bonuses, or provide a useful learning experience that will contribute some day to promotability, then their personal interests are aligned with the work. Or perhaps it is as simple as their being able to practice some skills they want to develop. Or to work in an area or on a project that they find interesting. There is usually some personal interest that can be found and aligned with the task. If not, well, then you need to talk it through and see if you can do something to make it more important and relevant for them.

There may be some interaction here between the organizational importance and the importance to the employee. For instance, most employees want to do work that matters to their organization because it is important for them to feel they are contributing.

There is often some way to link good work on even the dullest of tasks with some long-term aspiration of the employee. If all else fails, you can ask the classic "what do you want to be" or "where do you see yourself five years from now" questions, and then see if you can bundle anything into the work that contributes to that journey. Employees will often gladly take on some extra responsibilities in order to align work with their own aspirations.

For instance, let's say Joan hopes eventually to move out of her current department and into the marketing function. Maybe she would like to add a short report on sales and marketing activity or customer satisfaction or something marketing-oriented to her reports, so that she could gain some experience that might some day help her make a lateral move into marketing. There are often ways to negotiate the work at this stage to better align it with employee interests while still ensuring that the essential core results are produced.

Making Sure the Job Is Doable

The "HOW?" section of the planning form in Exhibit 6-2 looks at two sides of the question of ability. First, it asks you and the employee to identify the employee's performance requirements. Does the employee need to use a particular computer program? Need to know something about accounting? Need to create a spreadsheet? Need to call other departments and talk them into cooperating? There are always some skill requirements, and when you talk them through with the employee you can check that she is fully qualified to do the job. Often, it turns out that she may be a bit weak in some area and therefore the task is hard for her to do well. If so, then you have several options:

▶ You can provide help and support for her, either helping out yourself or asking another employee to help.

▶ You can give or arrange for some training, making sure that she acquires the needed skills and abilities.

▶ You can create reference materials, how-to guides, or other job aids.

▶ Or you can simply redesign the task so that it better fits her skill level.

One or a combination of these strategies will ensure a good fit between the employee's capabilities and the task at hand.

However, it takes more than a qualified employee to make the results fully attainable. There are often other resources the employee must depend upon. Identify what information, supplies, equipment, and help from others are essential for success, and make sure that they are available. If not, then help the employee line up the needed information, materials, help, or other needed resources. (For instance, Joan needs help in obtaining information from those uncooperative other departments before her reports are completely doable. As her manager, you need to know this, and to step in and help her get the information she needs. You may need to go to a manager in another department, explain the problem, and ask for help.)

The Final Step: A Learning Loop

No plan is ever perfect, no plan is ever complete. Dwight D. Eisenhower once expressed this point especially well when he remarked that "plans are nothing, planning is everything." The final step of any plan should therefore be a feedback loop or learning loop in which you stop to think about the plan and identify any weaknesses or remaining issues that you may want to revisit at a later date.

In the "ISSUES?" section of the planning form in Exhibit 6-2, you and the employee have an opportunity to list any remaining concerns. There may be things you could not fully resolve in your planning session. If so, don't worry too much about them—no doubt the task is better defined and more motivational now than when you started. But don't ignore the problems or concerns either, or you will never do any better. Take a moment to express any remaining concerns you may have, and also allow the employee to do the same. Note that this achieves some valuable communications goals even if you never do resolve those issues.

It also helps open up the communication channel between you and employees if you show them that you are willing to listen to their concerns. And it shows them that you take their concerns seriously enough to want to know what they are and even to take note of them—which demonstrates consideration on your part, a powerful technique for maintaining a healthy, positive emotional outlook on both your parts.

Then there is always the chance you can revisit the plan at a later date and find ways to resolve some of those issues. Management is after all a work in progress! So keep a copy of the planning form and let the employee keep one too. You can initiate another planning session when you feel it is appropriate—better sooner than later—and try to improve the plan.

Curious About "Job Enrichment"?

You may have wondered about Frederick Herzberg's concept of job enrichment, which was mentioned at the beginning of this chapter. But now that you've learned how to use the Motivational Task Plan Form, you have actually learned something about job enrichment. Herzberg found that when he redesigned jobs to make them into more whole and meaningful units of work, the employees were more motivated and performed better. In other words, he maximized the purpose aspect of the work, and thus made the work more likely to satisfy the employee's need for achievement.

Herzberg did some important studies in factory and office situations, in which employees were often doing repetitive, production-line tasks. He found that they often were more motivated and worked harder when their tasks were expanded vertically—in other words, when what they did spanned a larger piece of the entire production process. Instead of, say, only putting some bolts into a door panel, perhaps the workers would now assemble the entire door and hang it on the car. More and harder work, but more satisfying because you can see that you are actually building something important. You aren't just a "cog in the machine" but are actually crafting a significant part of the overall product.

When you talk through the what and why questions with your employees, you may well find yourself allowing them to stretch in this same way, so that they get to do something more meaningful and important. As long as you make sure the how question is answered and they have the ability to succeed, this is fine.

What About Meaningless Tasks?

The other thing you may find when you dig into specific tasks and duties is that some of them cannot be made to pass the opportunity test. There is little you can do to make some duties important. No matter how hard you and the employee try, some tasks will simply continue to appear trivial.

That's okay. In fact it is a wonderful discovery! Whenever you find out that something is not very important, then you can take time and resources away from it and shift them to something that *is* important. If you originated the assignment yourself and then discover it is not contributing to any important goal, well, you can simply drop it and put the employee on something more important. If on the other hand you inherited the assignment—it was assigned from above or is a part of a long-standing policy or tradition that you cannot change at the moment—well, you can still make sure that it does not drain too much energy from your people. One of the options for filling in the WHY? section in the Motivational Task Plan Form (for both organization and individual) is: "Get this requirement out of the way quickly so as to minimize the amount of time and energy it takes from more important tasks." That itself is a compelling purpose and well worth pursuing!

Managing the Destination

The process of exploring each major task with each employee helps you make sure that the employee (and you) understand the task, see why it is important, and clear the employee's path to successful completion. This focus on the task helps make it into a more inherently motivating opportunity to succeed. Many employees are disengaged, uncertain of what exactly they should be doing, or lacking the resources to do it right. So managing the tasks carefully is an important role for you as a manager, and it will significantly improve employees' connection with their work. But still it may not be sufficient to give all your people a strong sense of purpose and get them excited about their work.

The problem is that sometimes there is a broader lack of purpose in the workplace. If your organization is not clearly focused on a well-articulated plan or goal that excites you and your people, then it can be difficult to maintain a strong sense of purpose in individual tasks. And as a manager, you will sometimes find yourself working in organizations that seem to be in flux or to lack momentum or vision. In fact, most organizations do go through such phases. And you may not be in a position of sufficient authority to drive a new and compelling vision into place for the organization as a whole.

So the pragmatic thing to do is to give some thought to what sort of goal or plan you can articulate for your own group of employees—something that is exciting to you and gives extra purpose to your group's work, but which of course is not incompatible with the goals of the broader organization. (You don't want to get everyone fired up about an impractical plan and then have to backpedal when the rug is pulled out from under you.) In general, the easiest way to find a compelling vision or purpose for your group is to focus on those broader success factors for your organization that you as a manager have the most effect upon, given your group's work or focus.

A CASE IN POINT

A manager of a post office decided to focus on improving customer satisfaction. He put together a team of employees, and they spent a couple of years figuring out how to make their customers really happy. They drew in lots of new customers and revitalized their post office. At the time the U.S. Postal Service was struggling with major issues throughout its vast system and under great pressure from Congress to become profitable.

Now, the postmaster in his small corner of the country could not directly fix that problem, but he could make his own post office run better. And by improving service he increased the usage of his post office and achieved breakeven in his own unit. Later on, the postal service flew him around the country to explain how he had done it, proving that even one manager in one small area of an organization can make a big difference if he or she makes the personal commitment to do so.

By the way, if you cannot think of any other compelling goal to give more of a sense of purpose to your people, simply set a quality goal. Whatever you and your people do, it can always be done better. And if it is important, if it contributes to the bottom line in any way, or if it helps make customers happy, then doing it better will help the organization—often to a surprising degree.

But as you work on developing a quality improvement goal, remember to use your motivational communication skills discussed in Chapter 4. Engage your people as you develop and refine your ideas. Challenge them to think of ways to do the work better. Try to get them to identify the most important things to improve upon. That way, you'll get a meaningful and realistic goal, not just some arbitrary imposition by management that employees resent.

I am reminded of a story about a company that decided it needed to answer customer telephone calls more quickly in order to keep its customers from growing impatient. A manager arbitrarily set the quality goal of answering all calls before the fourth ring. To make sure employees took the goal seriously, the company's phone system was configured to count the number of rings—and employee bonuses and other rewards were tied to the goal. Now employees had to answer the phones within three rings or bad things would happen. And if they succeeded, they could win rewards for their success. A classic case of imposing a seemingly arbitrary goal and then using strong extrinsic motivators to make employees do it.

You can guess what happened—especially when I tell you the company did not hire more employees or give the current employees any help in handling calls more quickly. Employees simply learned to pick up each phone call by the third ring—even if this meant they had to hang up on another customer or that they had to leave the phone off the hook so the new caller waited endlessly. The three-ring goal was achieved, all right, but customer service got far worse instead of better.

What Is Your Most Compelling Goal?

As a manager, you need to have a "big-picture" view of where you want to lead your people. What do you want them to do that will be worth remembering and telling their friends about next year or ten years from now? What one thing will you all look back on with the greatest pride and sense of accomplishment? Yet the daily crush of routine work can make it difficult to pay attention to such long-term concerns. Sometimes managers go for years without ever having more of a vision than simply surviving another week!

So take this moment to think about your current work situation (or one you will soon be in if you expect to advance to a higher level of management in the near future). Stop and think about what you would like to accomplish. Then *articulate a single, clear goal that you can share with your people to give special meaning and pride of achievement to their daily work.*

It is a surprisingly difficult exercise, and one you may want to revisit and revise in the future. But the important thing is to make sure you stop and ask yourself this key question and make the effort to focus on a *destination* for your management journey.

Avoiding Extremes: The Right Level of Challenge

As you manage your people's opportunities, you need to be aware of the relationship between level of difficulty and motivation. Opportunities that are too difficult are simply not motivating. In fact they are demotivating. So be careful to make sure that the work you ask people to do is truly doable for them. Employees seldom feel it is appropriate to express their fears or anxieties or lack of understanding, so you have to ask. You have to probe with lots of open questions until you are fairly sure you have assessed the level of difficulty from their perspective and know that it is not "over the top" and too difficult in their eyes. If it is, it doesn't necessarily mean they can't do it. But it does mean you need to make sure they get some support, instruction, simplified step-by-step assignments, or initial help from you or another more experienced employee. There are many ways to reduce the difficulty level—once you realize that's what you need to do.

As Exhibit 6-3 shows, there is actually an interestingly complex relationship between level of difficulty and motivation. It turns out that people are highly motivated at moderate levels of difficulty—and not motivated at levels that are either too high or too low.

Why? The demotivating effects of excessively high difficulty are fairly obvious. If you don't see how you can possibly achieve a goal, then you are not going to be motivated to try. If you are forced by your boss to try, you will experience high anxiety, stress, and fear of failure. So it makes good sense that too high levels of difficulty hurt motivation and destroy the good effects of opportunities.

But what about the opposite situation, where something is so easy it is trivial and presents no real challenge to you? Do you feel good when you do something really easy? No. There is no pride, no

EXHIBIT 6-3. Managing the level of difficulty.

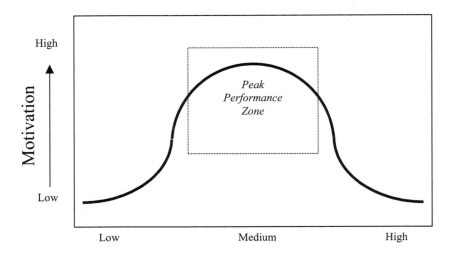

Level of Difficulty

sense of achievement, no glow of victory. You wouldn't want to play a game that was so easy you could win 100 percent of the time without really trying. Nobody would make such a game their favorite hobby. Nor would you want to do work that is mindlessly easy. Yet too often, that is just what employees do. They do some repetitive, routine task that they have done a thousand times before. They are no longer paying any real attention to the job, if they ever did in the first place. They are just going through the motions.

So as a manager, you need to be on your guard for employees who have slipped into a dull routine and are not challenged at all by their work. This is just as demotivating as too high a level of challenge. Either situation flunks the opportunity quiz we used earlier in the chapter (remember *purpose, interest,* and *ability*?). Too little challenge and you kill the interest. Too much challenge and you destroy the ability. So make sure you manage the level of challenge in order to bring out the incredible motivational power of good opportunities.

Summary

The key point to remember from this chapter is that opportunities to succeed at something important are highly motivational. *They stimulate intrinsic motivation* (when viewed from a positive emotional framework—see Chapter 5) and are therefore a powerful lever for motivational management. Yet most employees do not have meaningful, exciting challenges to pursue in their work—or if they do, they lack needed skills or resources to do so. To harness the power of opportunity, you need to make sure your employees are focused on doing important work and that they have the ability to do it well. Then their natural desire to achieve will kick in and give them a high level of motivation.

You can introduce a compelling goal like improving quality as a way to give a higher sense of purpose to your employees. You can also give employees new or modified tasks that provide greater opportunities for achievement. To transform their duties into more motivational opportunities to succeed, make sure each employee is doing work that has a clear purpose, is interesting to them, and is doable—both in terms of their capabilities and in terms of their access to needed information, materials, teamwork, or other necessary resources.

Also make sure that employees are operating at an optimal level of challenge. Any employees who are struggling with overly difficult or unattainable goals need to be given help or support or step-by-step instructions to follow. And employees who are bored and not being stretched to achieve challenging results need to be given greater challenges. Introduce stretch goals for them, and their motivation will increase.

CHAPTER 7

Using Feedback to Motivate

How often do you see a stadium that has no scoreboard? Knowing how you are doing is an essential part of playing any organized sport. Yet sometimes (too often, to be honest), employees play the great game of work without visible scoreboards. That is a problem, or perhaps an opportunity—an opportunity for motivational management to enhance performance in yet another powerful way!

Feedback is information about employees' performance that they can use to improve the results and/or the underlying process. Notice that this definition of feedback emphasizes the *usefulness* of the information. It helps employees make improvements to their performance. That is the purpose of feedback. That is why managers value feedback. But much of what passes as feedback in the workplace fails this simple test. It does not help people do a better job.

Useful Information

Imagine that Francine's boss sees her in the hall one day and says, "Oh, Francine, I wanted to tell you that some of the other people on the Special Projects Team are not happy with your performance. They say you don't put enough effort in. Can you try to carry a little more weight on the team projects from now on? Thanks, I appreciate it." Is this true feedback or not?

Well, I don't know how you answered the question, but to my eye it is difficult to say for sure until we find out whether Francine's performance improved as a result of the information. If it didn't, then it was not feedback by our strict improvement-oriented definition. But if it did, well, then it worked, which makes it effective—and that makes it feedback.

You may be saying, yes, but was it *good* feedback? *I* wouldn't like to have a boss talk to me that way.

I agree. It was an inconsiderate comment, and Francine's manager probably needs to read this book or one like it. If I were Francine, I might very well feel that my boss is just passing on an unkind rumor and not giving me a chance to defend myself. It would have been a lot better if Francine's boss had tried using some open questions instead of just telling her what he thought she should do.

But let's just say that both Francine and her boss know that she has been ducking work on the team projects and not trying nearly as hard as her teammates. And let's furthermore imagine that Justine did not realize her boss took the team project that seriously. And now that she knows it is important, she will put more effort into it. Those are admittedly a lot of assumptions, but if we accept them as true, then perhaps the comment from her boss does qualify as feedback. As long as it effects an improvement in her behavior, it works—and it's feedback.

But let's also be clear on another important point. *Not all feedback is equal.* Some feedback works much, much better than other feedback. There is a surprisingly large range of effectiveness, which means that managers who develop the art of feedback are able to achieve far more than those who don't. Francine's manager is not a skilled user of feedback. You can do far better.

Good Feedback Makes Excellence More Visible

In this chapter, we will explore the art of feedback by, first, understanding how you can design it so as to help employees see their work more clearly. And second, we will look at several levels or stages of feedback to see how you can move from basic to more advanced (and effective) forms over time with your people.

As the definition of feedback points out, the purpose of feed-back is to help the employees improve their performance. Feedback needs to contribute to learning. It can do this in a simple way, by allowing employees to fix a result, and it can also contribute in a more sophisticated way by helping employees learn to improve the work process that *produced* the result. Feedback also contributes to learning when it confirms that a work method and result are successful, so that the employees knows to continue working in that manner. (Exhibit 7-1 shows these two options graphically.)

The more easily the employee can interpret these forms of feed-back and use them to learn about the quality of results and work methods, the better. Feedback that makes the nature and quality of

EXHIBIT 7-1. The impact of feedback on employee performance. ───────

Productive Impacts on Employee Performance

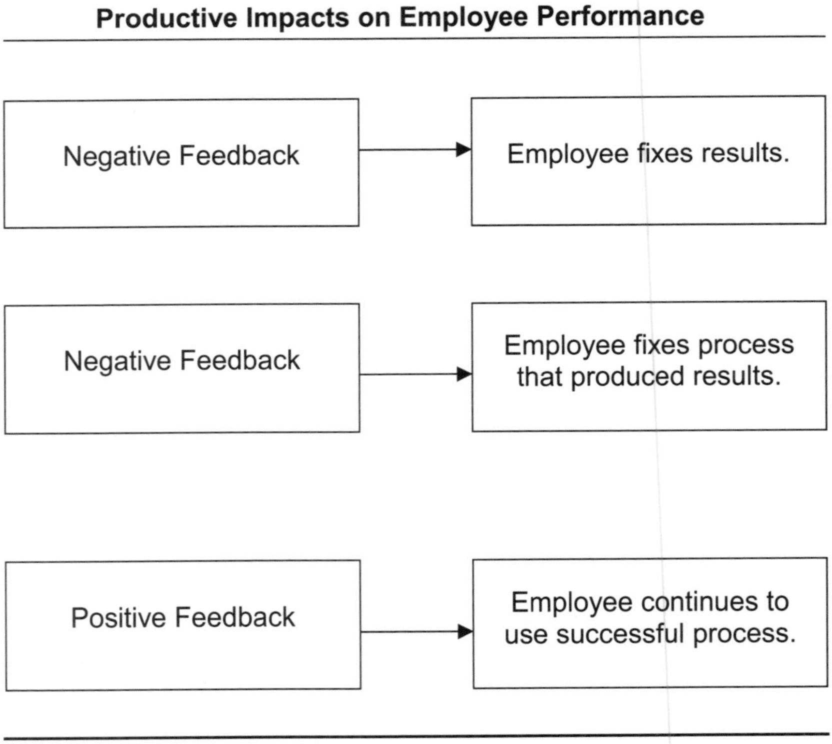

your work methods and results more visible is most likely to prove useful. The more visible that feedback makes the work, the more valuable it is in improving the quality of work and the more it appeals to the employee's intrinsic desire to achieve successful results.

Let's do a little exercise to help explore this issue of feedback's role in making quality of work more visible.

Exercise 7-1. How helpful is this feedback?

Imagine you are an employee of a consulting firm who interacts with many customers, both in person and by telephone and e-mail. Your company is introducing an initiative to improve customer service with the goal of retaining customers for longer. As a result, you have recently received a variety of feedback about customer service:

▶ Your boss told you that she'd heard some complaints about you from a couple of customers last quarter, but didn't specify which customers or exactly what the complaints were about.

▶ The marketing department issued a survey report indicating that customers of your company rated the quality of customer service at 87 percent overall.

▶ The president of the company sent an e-mail to all employees discussing the importance of customer relationships and asking everyone to try to be more polite and helpful to clients and prospects in the future.

Looking over this list of feedback, think about how useful it is in improving your own performance. How valuable is this feedback in helping you make specific improvements in the results of your work, or in the basic approach and work process by which you produce your results? Identify specific things that you can see need to be changed:

| |
| |

```
┌─────────────────────────────────────────────┐
│                                             │
├─────────────────────────────────────────────┤
│                                             │
└─────────────────────────────────────────────┘
```

Sample Solution

Have trouble coming up with anything to write down? I'm not surprised. This is a trick question, and there *are* no good answers. The information you received is not really very clear. All it tells you is that management is increasingly uptight about customer service. But none of your feedback is specific enough to show you *what* to do or *how* to improve.

Unfortunately, much of the feedback that managers give employees is similar to the feedback listed in the exercise—and is too vague to be of much practical use. It is easy to fall into the trap of restating the goal over and over rather than providing informative feedback to help people figure out how to achieve that goal.

As Exercise 7-1 illustrates, well-intentioned feedback is not necessarily as useful and productive as managers intend. When it comes to management, good intentions aren't nearly enough!

What is necessary for feedback to be more effective? How can you ensure that your employees receive feedback that makes their methods and results more visible to them and easier to improve? One of the best answers to these questions is to make sure the feedback maximizes *task clarity*.

Maximizing the Clarity of Feedback

Feedback clarity expresses how clearly you can see the *links* from what you do to the results you achieve. Feedback provides the most clarity when it is:

> ▶ *Specific* (so employee can relate it to identifiable behaviors or actions)

> ▶ *Accurate* (so it leads to helpful insights, not confusion or anger)

▶ *Informative* (so as to give insight into how to do things differently and better)

▶ *Controllable* (so it relates to behaviors or actions the *employee* can change)

For example, imagine you tell an employee that the last time he spoke with a customer by telephone, he had told them that he would look up some information and send it to them, but then he forgot to follow up. This feedback is very specific, it is accurate, it is informative, and it is presumably controllable, since the employee himself is responsible for completing the task and could come up with a better method for noting and tracking such promises. So the feedback you give this employee provides high task clarity. It makes the links between employee performance and results more visible to the employee. *It helps them see their own performance more clearly.*

In contrast, much of the feedback employees receive is too vague to provide clarity. To see this for yourself, take another look at the feedback statements from Exercise 7-1. They are reproduced in Exercise 7-2, this time with a checklist for evaluating them in terms of their clarity.

Exercise 7-2. Applying the Clarity Test.

Take a look at the following three examples of feedback and check to see how many of the four clarity criteria each one meets.

Examples of Feedback	Clarity Test
1. Your boss told you that she'd heard some complaints about you from a couple of customers last quarter, but didn't specify which customers or exactly what the complaints were about.	Specific? Accurate? Informative? Controllable?

---

2. The marketing department issued a survey re-   Specific?
   port indicating that customers of your company   Accurate?
   rated the quality of customer service at 87 per- Informative?
   cent overall.   Controllable?

---

3. The president of the company sent an e-mail to   Specific?
   all employees discussing the importance of cus- Accurate?
   tomer relationships and asking everyone to try   Informative?
   to be more polite and helpful to clients and pros- Controllable?
   pects in the future.

Sample Solutions

The first feedback example might be controllable, since it is about your individual performance. But it is not specific or informative enough to be of much
use.

The second example is not specific (since it is about overall customer
perceptions and not the specific actions that produce them). Its accuracy is
damaged by the time delay in generating survey data too. (How long does it
take to survey customers and produce a report? Usually months and
months.) It does not give you information with enough detail to qualify as
informative (what should you do different? It's not clear). Nor is this feedback
controllable (since it is about the entire company's performance, not your
individual performance).

The third example of feedback, the president's memo, is even less specific, informative, or controllable. None of these do well on the feedback
clarity test.

Good Intentions

The three examples of well-intentioned but unhelpful feedback in
Exercise 7-2 fail to be specific, accurate, informative, and controllable enough to truly provide useful information. Most managers are
not very good at evaluating the feedback they give and do not realize its flaws, so this exercise is a useful one for anyone to do. As a
manager, you need to provide much more behavior-specific, helpful

feedback for your people. Make sure they know what the results are from specific things they do, make sure they see results quickly enough to be useful, and try to help them separate out and focus on their own personal impact and what to do differently next time.

To achieve these goals and pass the feedback clarity test, you can use a variety of feedback methods and strategies, which will be covered in the remainder of this chapter. They are divided into three levels, as most managers find it easier to think of them and learn them in sequence rather than all at once.

Level One: Positive and Negative Feedback

Ken Blanchard (of *One Minute Manager* fame) is particularly adamant about the importance of "catching someone doing something right." He points out that managers too easily fall into what he calls the "leave alone—zap" pattern of management, in which they do not pay much attention to employees until there is a problem. From the employee's perspective, it seems like their manager is just there to catch them doing something wrong—and zap them with negative feedback when they do.

Turning Performance Around with Recognition

Consultant Ferdinand Fournies recounts the story of a manager who turned around a problematic employee by deciding to recognize anything good he did rather than continue to keep focusing on what he did wrong. He quotes the manager as saying that "I started to praise him for the right things he did" and "In the past I would always wait until he had finished his assignment before going over it with him. I find now by showing him more interest in his work and by the combination of praise and lack of negative comments, his productivity has risen dramatically." This employee still isn't perfect, but he is at least improving. And all because the manager decided to start recognizing improvement and giving ongoing supportive feedback. It's amazing how much difference a small change of perspective can make.

It is too easy to fall into the habit of ignoring employee performance until something goes wrong. But if you do, you will find yourself giving a lot more negative feedback than positive feedback. And how does it feel to get mostly negative feedback from your manager? Let's find out.

A CASE IN POINT: THE NEW SALESMAN

Take the case of Ralph, who recently took a job as a salesman for a high-tech company. The product is complex, Ralph does not know the territory very well, and there are lots of ways to mess up. But he is trying hard to make the job a success and putting in very long days. His sales manager is quite busy (like most managers), but because she knows Ralph needs a little extra attention in this start-up period, she makes a point of reviewing his numbers and checking up on his more important customers at least once a week. For the last two months, she has been mentioning or writing memos about any problems or errors she sees so that Ralph can correct them and learn what is expected of him. Of course, since he is in the field most days, Ralph rarely interacts with his boss. Most weeks, the one or two corrections she gives him are his only communications he has with her.

Ralph's boss does not feel like she is being negative toward him. She only corrects his performance once a week, after all, not every day. And she is giving him a lot of autonomy and responsibility for a new employee because she feels he is exceptionally able and will quickly learn the ropes.

But what is Ralph's perspective? He looks back over the first couple of months on the job, and what he recalls is a long series of negative comments from his boss. And because he views them as critical, he of course remembers every one. Nobody is so thick-skinned that they can take criticism lightly, after all! So Ralph's recollection of his feedback from his boss is that it is almost 100 percent negative.

He naturally concludes that she does not like his work. He feels that the new job is not going well. He thinks he is off to a bad start. In fact, by now (after a string of eight or ten of these negative interactions), Ralph suspects he is the wrong man for the job and that he probably shouldn't have rushed to accept the first serious offer that came his way.

He is discouraged, and his motivation is falling. All because—from his perspective—his boss does not like his work. That's the problem with negative feedback. And that's why it is very important to balance it, in fact to *over*balance it, with positive feedback.

According to Ken Blanchard, for every time you correct an employee, you should tell them they are doing it right at least three times. That's a good ratio to try to keep in mind when you find yourself in the role of having to provide direct feedback to employees about their performances.

Watch Out for "Sandwich" Feedback

Supervisor and management trainings usually teach the sandwich method of correcting performance. First, they advise, you should tell employees that they are valuable or good at their work or have great potential. Next, you should give them the specific negative feedback—what you want them to correct or do better next time. Finally, to complete the sandwich, you should give them another bit of praise, usually referring to their potential value to the company and how you hope they will live up to it (by following the advice in the middle of the sandwich, of course).

I've always wondered about the wisdom of this technique, because it doesn't feel very good when someone uses it on me. (And besides, nobody really eats sandwiches that have good bread but bad-tasting filling, at least not by choice.) Because this feels like a fairly manipulative and controlling approach to me, I was interested to read the following quote in *Bringing Out the Best in People*, by Aubrey Daniels: "Some psychologists say this method preserves one's self-esteem in the process of correcting. I know of no experimental data that demonstrates that fact. I think it helps the punisher—not the punished."

Daniels is a Ph.D. industrial psychologist, so I think we can take his word on this one. Unfortunately, it turns out we've been teaching and using a technique that doesn't work. But the good news is, there are always alternative approaches to try! Perhaps the best one is to simply provide clear, informative, and accurate negative feedback, unadorned by fancy packaging. If the news is bad, tell it like it is and get it over with.

Good Start—But Let's Take This to a Higher Level

The idea of you as a manager watching over your employees and telling them when they do well or poorly is fine—as a beginning. It is appropriate when you are orienting an employee to a new task for which they need help and practice. It is appropriate if you have not yet had the time to create a feedback system that makes the employee more self-sufficient. But it is a highly directive way to manage.

You really don't want to have to stand at every employee's shoulder giving directions. And they certainly don't want you looking over their shoulder all the time either. In truth, in a healthy organization the *minority* of the feedback should come from you and other managers. Most of it should come from systems and scoreboards you put in place—or even better, that you help the employees create so they can monitor their own performances. Let's see how that can be done.

Level Two: From Controlling to Informative Feedback

The reason it is important to take feedback to a higher level is that it will help you inspire the intrinsic motivation of your employees. If your employees wait for you to inspect or review their work, and then for you to give them positive or negative feedback, this leaves them quite dependent on you. Your feedback is an extrinsic motivator. They rely on your judgement, and they tend to work to *please you*. I sometimes call that stop-light management, since it feels like your negative feedback is the red light and your positive feedback is the green light. And the question is, do you as a manager want to have to stand around playing the role of a traffic light all your working life? Probably not!

Traditional feedback is termed *controlling feedback* because it tends to rely on the manager's judgment, and the employee stops and goes in response to it. In other words, it is used to control performances, not to inspire them. But if you don't want to be a stop-light manager, what is the alternative?

The opposite of controlling feedback is *informative feedback*. It gives employees enough information to decide for them*selves* whether the work is good or bad. It transfers the information on which you as a manager would base your judgement, giving it to the employees so that they can be a better judge of their own performance. Informative feedback shifts the decision-making from the manager to the employee. And that tends to stimulate intrinsic motivation, which turns the employees on and lets you off the hook so you can stop directing traffic and do something more important with your time!

The idea of informative feedback is quite simple, but it can be surprisingly difficult to implement. So an example might be helpful. Let's say that you run a regional audit department for an accounting firm and you manage employees who perform audits and then write up reports for each client. As the manager, you keep a close eye on the quality of the work and also try to make sure it is done in a timely manner. You often find yourself going over a report and making corrections or raising questions. And you sometimes have to point out to your people that a client has been waiting too long and needs their report finished right away. In other words, you have to provide negative feedback—flash a red light—when something goes wrong. To balance this, you try to make a point of congratulating employees when they do an especially good job on an audit. But how can you switch from controlling to more informative feedback to encourage employees to catch their own errors and increase their speed?

For starters, you could stop pointing out specific errors and instead create a list of the types of errors you tend to find in reports—and then ask employees to check their reports for those errors before they submit them to you. The list of common types of errors and how to recognize them is a powerful example of informative feedback.

Second, you could also introduce the practice of counting how many of each type of error are found and corrected in audits. This creates a benchmark for tracking the sloppiness of report writing. And if employees keep an eye on the measure, they may be encouraged to find ways to learn to avoid errors in the first place.

Third, you could also ask the employees to track the time it takes them to write each report, and perhaps you could set a goal for turning reports around (such as two weeks) and also have them track how many reports exceed this time goal.

Now you have got several types of informative feedback at work, supplementing your policing efforts and *creating scoreboards that the employees can judge their own performance against*. I sometimes think of the results of good informative feedback as employee scoreboards, in contrast to the more mindless traffic lights you get with controlling styles of feedback.

Exercise 7-3. Recognizing controlling vs. informative feedback.

Take a minute to review each of the following feedback statements and then check which are informative and which are controlling:

1. "Good start, but don't forget you need to close out all of the day's transactions before leaving too."
   - ❏ Controlling?
   - ❏ Informative?
2. "Have you reviewed the checklist we use when we close out for the day? It's posted over there."
   - ❏ Controlling?
   - ❏ Informative?

3. "I like the work you did on that last report, Joan. Your effort is really appreciated!"
   - ❏ Controlling?
   - ❏ Informative?
4. "I went over the last report and found half as many errors as usual."
   - ❏ Controlling?
   - ❏ Informative?
5. "It looks like the errors we are finding in your reports are mostly simple typos and spelling errors. Can you run a spell checker on them before you submit them for review?"
   - ❏ Controlling?
   - ❏ Informative?

Solution

1 = controlling
2 = informative
3 = controlling
4 = controlling
5 = informative

Remember that any feedback that encourages employees to rely on your judgment of their work is controlling (whether positive or negative). And any feedback that helps employees make an informed judgement of their own is informative (whether positive or negative).

Level Three: Codesigning Feedback Systems

Going from level-one feedback (a good mix of positive and negative feedback) to level-two feedback (more informative and less controlling) is a big step for most managers. It takes some effort and practice to do it well—for employees as well as their managers. And there will still be times when level-one approaches are the best alternative, at least until you can think of ways of putting scorecard-style information in the employee's hands. So why take it to yet another level?

Because you will find as you get used to providing more informative feedback that, while the employees rely less on your *judgment*, they may still be relying heavily on your *information*. And
to make them even more self-sufficient and even more intrinsically
motivated, you will want to establish information systems that allow
the employees to generate their *own* informative feedback. So yet
another distinction becomes useful, this one between manager-
generated and employee-generated feedback. And as a manager,
you will find it desirable (good for employee attitudes and performances) to work on creating feedback systems that allow employees
to *generate and track their own information about their performances*. Taking feedback to this third level makes employees even
more independent and intrinsically motivated.

Feedback That Takes You Out of the Loop

The key to good feedback systems is that they take you, the manager, out of the loop. For example, consider the difference between
these two scenarios:

A. You review audit reports before they are sent to customers,
flagging any errors you find and sending them back to employees to fix.

B. Employees use an audit review checklist to go over each other's reports and make corrections. You only check the occasional random report to make sure the system is working.

In option A you do a lot more work. In option B the employees
are a lot more self-sufficient. They are generating more of their own
feedback. Much of the time, they find errors and correct them before you have to get involved. You can see how that is better for
you as the manager, and also how it tends to appeal to employees'
intrinsic motivation to do a good job. As long as they can see why it
is important to catch and correct errors—that is, as long as there is a
visible and appealing purpose—these employees should catch most
errors without your help.

A Feedback Design Process

In the example above, the employees are using a participatory and informative feedback system. Such systems can be difficult to create. They take insight and imagination. And if you do all the work of designing such systems, they are not only a burden on you but they can seem somewhat arbitrary and controlling to employees. So the best way to create informative feedback systems is to codesign them with your employees. Here is a process you can use:

1. *Specify a clear goal and a good reason for pursuing it.* For example, your goal might be to have employees be nicer to customers (a goal) so that customer turnover will be minimized (a good reason). Discuss the goal with the employee(s) and agree on it, then write it down.

2. *Think of many ways of making progress toward the goal visible, trackable, measurable.* For example, you and your employees might think of using a customer satisfaction survey, asking customers during the call if they are happy with the service or if there is anything they need, measuring and graphing customer turnover, keeping track of how many times you remember to smile when you are on the phone with a customer, tracking each customer request/question and whether it was handled as the customer wanted or not, and so forth. There are always lots of possibilities but it takes an effort to stop and think about some of them.

3. *Agree on one to several good measures or methods, then assign responsibility for implementing them.* For example, your employees might agree to keep note of customer requests and how each is resolved. You could ask for a volunteer to create a form for tracking them, and then you could take responsibility for asking everyone to share their results in the weekly staff meetings from now on.

4. *Check the system periodically to make sure it is on target, working, and can't be improved upon.* For example, you

might decide after a few months that the system is helpful, but is too difficult to do on paper. So you and your people decide to upgrade it to a spreadsheet to save time.

This process is participatory and designed to encourage employees to become more involved in designing and managing their own feedback systems. It is a pretty sophisticated approach to feedback management. But then again, maximizing employee motivation and performance is a pretty sophisticated undertaking, so it might be wise to practice these skills before moving on.

Designing Feedback for Joan

Let's revisit Joan, the star of several earlier chapters, and focus once again on her report-writing duties.

It has come to the attention of her manager (that's you) that Joan sometimes turns in reports late. You don't know how often this happens, but you do know that when it does, it inconveniences the accounting department, which relies on those reports to update customer accounts and do their invoicing and collections. Not only that, but if the reports are late, then presumably invoicing and collections are affected, slowing down the flow of cash to the firm and affecting the bottom line as a result. So on-time completion of reports is an important goal. But just complaining to Joan that the accounting department says she is often late is not a particularly effective approach to feedback. (It is controlling—dependent on you, and of course it is negative and "catches her doing something wrong," which will tend to be discouraging to Joan.) So what can you do to take it to a higher level?

Using the Feedback Design Process, you plan to meet with Joan to go over the goal and explain its purpose and importance. Then you intend to ask her to cooperate in creating some kind of feedback mechanism to help track the timeliness of reports and to give her and the rest of her report-writing associates something to judge performance against. Before the meeting begins, you want to have some ideas of your own in case Joan does not come up with ones you like. That way, you can make some suggestions or ask questions to guide her to a good approach.

Exercise 7-4. Tracking reports.

Come up with three alternative approaches to measuring and tracking the timeliness of reports:

1.

2.

3.

Now you are ready to get Joan (or any employee) thinking productively about how to track on-time performance.

Exercise 7-4 asked you to apply some management imagination to the challenge of how to measure and track on-time performance for Joan's report-writing duties. Specifically, it asked you to generate three alternative approaches. Why?

The Need for Imagination

It is important to look at and think about multiple alternatives whenever you develop a feedback system. In Chapter 6 we read about the manager who wanted to reduce customer frustration with his department's phone service by specifying that all calls had to be answered by the third ring. He then had the phone system programmed to count the number of calls answered by the third ring and the number answered later than that. Perfect performance was defined as no calls going past the third ring.

I bet that was his first idea for how to measure and track the speed of phone service. It turned out to be a bad idea, since employees hung up on customers and cut calls short in order to make their numbers. If he had thought harder about it, and had asked employees to generate some suggestions too, then he might have hit upon a better feedback system. He needed to measure and track something that was more closely aligned with the quality of the customer's telephone experience, something that captured the big picture and not just one aspect of it. Any ideas?

How about this? What he really wanted to do was to encourage employees to make sure each caller felt like he or she was getting good service. So really, what needs to be measured is an overall indicator of the customer's perception of how good service was for each call. Either this would have to be defined in terms of a number of quantitative measures (such as hold time, whether employee could answer the question, how long it takes for the employee transaction, and so forth), or it could be measured with a judgmental scale such as:

How happy was this customer with our level of service? Customer sounded:
1 = Very unhappy
2 = Unhappy
3 = In the middle, neutral
4 = Happy
5 = Very happy

The advantage of this scale is that it captures the customer's overall impression, rather than trying to boil it down to one or a few easy-to-measure aspects of the call. Of course this scale is a bit harder to capture—the phone system won't do it automatically. But the manager could ask each employee to rate each call as best they can. And then the company could do an occasional telephone survey of customers to get some data from their perspective for comparison.

It is a completely different approach to performance feedback from measuring the number of rings, and it might do a better job of producing improvements in customer service. But perhaps there is an even better way. Who knows? The quality of your feedback systems is only limited by your imagination—and your willingness to apply it to this important aspect of your work.

A Solution to Exercise 7-4

By now you may be wondering whether your three answers in Exercise 7-4 are on target or not. In general, if you have thought about it hard enough to have three different alternatives, you are far ahead of most managers, so *any* answers are good ones. (It is a brainstorming exercise, and in brainstorming, quantity leads to quality, not the other way around.) But to give you some further insight into the exercise, here are several ideas that might work reasonably well as ways of tracking the on-time delivery of reports:

1. Simply count the number of reports that are delivered on time and the number delivered late. If your objective is to deliver them all on time, then you can celebrate each time you deliver ten (or some such number) on time. And you will also get accurate and clear negative feedback in the form of a number representing how many reports were turned in late each week and month.

2. You could refine the measure by calculating the percentage of reports turned in on time. For example, if your department produces twenty reports in a month and five of them are late, then the on-time performance is 15/20, or 75 percent. Using this as a benchmark, you would get positive feedback in the following month if the rate went up to, say, 80 percent. You could also set a goal by, for example, saying that you want the department to work on achieving a 95 percent on-time rate by the sixth month of measuring this statistic. (And you could also ask individual employees to

track their own on-time rates. If Joan is doing better than the department-wide rate of 75 percent, then she can feel good about her performance, and you can reassure the accounting department that she is a relatively fast report writer.)

3. You might find that once reports are late, they tend to get later and later. Once late, employees have no incentive to hand them in quickly—since in the two systems above they are only counted as late once. So an alternative that would avoid this problem is to keep a running total of the number of "late report days," which you could define as the sum of the number of days each report is late. (For example, if Joan has one report that is three days late, and two other employees have five-day-late reports, then the department-wide late report days statistic would be thirteen late report days (3 + 5 + 5). Again, you could ask individual employees to track their own numbers, and also pool them for the department as a whole.

In addition to these three ideas, here is a fourth alternative, completely different from the other three. You could call your contacts in the accounting department once a month and ask them to rate the on-time delivery of reports, and also ask for an overall quality rating, using scales such as these:

▶ "In the past month, what grade would you give our department for timeliness of reports? Use a percentage scale, from 0 percent to 100 percent."

▶ "In the past month, what grade would you give our department for overall quality of reports? Again, please use a percentage scale, from 0 percent to 100 percent."

Then you could report these statistics to your employees, and maybe even post them on a chart for all to see.

If I actually had to manage Joan's department, I might choose to use two or even three of the measures, depending upon how important this goal is to me. (And I would certainly ask my employees to help me decide which ones to choose!) That way, I would have plenty of informative feedback systems in place. If you had to choose two measures from my list of four, which two would you choose? Why? How about from your own list in the exercise?

You Don't Have to Be a Slave to Praise

Should you *praise employees every day*? That's the current wisdom as the need to motivate employees gains urgency in businesses. From *Inc.* magazine comes the advice that supervisors should write a weekly "to do" list with each employee's name on it, to be crossed off when you find a way to praise them. A newsletter called *The Motivational Manager* prescribes even more frequent praise, recommending that every manager "make recognizing employees part of your daily routine."[1]

And many managers are getting the message these days—but feeling guilty because they don't have the time or inclination to be a full-time cheerleader for their people. Should you feel like you've failed your people when you don't provide continuous praisings? Is it essential to provide frequent, positive feedback for employees? No! Actually, these prescriptions are flawed, and if taken too seriously can backfire and hurt attitudes and performance.

It is a good idea to try to adjust the level of challenge so that employees get it right a lot more often than they get it wrong. A healthy ratio of positive to negative results is probably at least nine to one. People like to succeed most of the time—and if their work is important, you want your people to succeed. *But* that does not necessarily mean you have to be a full-time cheerleader. Being a glad-handing, back-patting slave to doling out recognition and rewards takes too much of your energy and time and does not feel sincere to your employees. As Samuel Johnson put it, he who praises everybody praises nobody.

If managers insert themselves into employees' daily work to tell them when they are doing well, employees will become more dependent upon managers' telling them they are doing well. They will become "hooked" on this external source of feedback. They will work for the praise. Too rich a diet of praise can be overly controlling. Employees tend to learn to look to their managers for approval, instead of developing independent judgment about what is and is not good work.

The same problem arises when you use "token" feedback systems, in which employees earn tokens, points, or credits when their managers think they are performing well. Better to emphasize informing and educating employees, with the goal of making them more independent instead of more dependent. Remember your goal is high *intrinsic* motivation, not extrinsic motivation.

Also, if your management plan makes praise the main source of positive feedback, you will inevitably provide inconsistent, arbitrary feedback. Why? Because managers cannot possibly watch employees closely enough to know exactly when they do what, let alone whether they've done a good or poor job at each task they do in a day. When managers do happen to take note of a good performance and praise it, the event is an anomaly that often takes employees by surprise. Employees may even feel that the praise is inappropriate or should have been directed at a much more important performance the manager is unaware of. Employees will find it difficult to predict or control the desirable praisings. And when they view praise as inconsistent and arbitrary, it is not motivating to them. They lack the clarity of understanding needed to relate their own performances to the desired outcome.

Another problem with focusing on praising your people is that it is really just one single, simple prescription for every individual and every situation. What motivates each individual? It depends on their personality, plus their current commitment and competence levels. A simple pat on the back, administered formulaically to each employee, is not appropriate for most of them. Same with many traditional reward systems and programs, which hand out generic reinforcers even though each employee's context and behavior is unique. There is no substitute for good one-on-one supervision. Employees know it. Managers need to admit it too.

In addition to these problems with daily praise, there is another simple consideration. Managers have precious little time to devote to each individual employee. If they are busy giving positive feedback each day, then they won't have any time to think about other important forms of feedback. They will certainly tend to overlook the vital distinction between informative and controlling feedback. And they will not have the time to help employees set appropriately challenging performance goals, and to work with them to develop and use their own measures to track their performances.

Summary

It is important to make sure your employees have a rich diet of feedback—information that they can use to improve their results and/or the work processes that produce those results. In giving feedback, try to make sure it passes the task clarity test: that it is specific, accurate, informative, and controllable. Also watch the mix of positive and negative feedback, remembering that too much negative feedback discourages employees and hurts motivation. And to maximize intrinsic motivation, try to take your feedback to the next level by providing as informative feedback as possible and avoiding feedback that makes employees overly dependent on your judgment.

Your goal should be to stimulate employees to improve their own judgment so they can monitor their own performances more effectively. And if you can, try taking feedback to an even higher level by using the Feedback Design Process. It engages employees in a creative effort to design the best informative feedback systems for monitoring their own work. If you bring feedback to a higher level, you will not feel stuck with having to be a constant cheerleader for your people. You do not need to spend all your time correcting errors and trying to find excuses to praise. Instead, you need to manage performance through participatory, informative feedback systems that have high task clarity—and so are ideal for helping employees excel in their work.

Notes

1. *The Motivational Manager*, undated issue received May 1998 from Ragan Communications, Chicago, Ill., p.1.

CHAPTER 8

Eliminating
Contaminants

> So much of what we call manage-
> ment consists in making it difficult
> for people to work.
>
> —Peter Drucker

I sometimes show my own audiences two pictures—one of a wild horse running free, the other of a saddled horse carrying a rider. And I ask, which one is going to run faster and farther, the one with the heavy harness, saddle, and rider to carry, or the one that is free? Well, it depends a lot on the rider and the rider's relationship with the horse, doesn't it? We can imagine situations in which the horse with the rider might perform better in spite of having to carry that extra weight. But we can also imagine the wild horse winning the race, at least if it has a mind to. The rider is obviously an added burden. So too are managers. To make up for their extra weight, they need to actively contribute in many ways to the performance of their organization. It is not always easy to avoid the trap Peter Drucker refers to in the opening quote, in which the manager makes it difficult for people to work instead of easier.

In this chapter, we're going to take a hard look at the more common ways in which managers most often damage performance instead of helping it. This is not as much fun as the other chapters, since it can feel a bit critical. Sorry! It is necessary, however, to make sure we are not demotivating anyone by accident. An ounce of de-motivation needs a pound of motivation to cancel it out, so it's much better to eliminate potential contaminants to employees' healthy attitudes rather than let them weigh down our corporate saddle bags.

One of the easiest ways to slow a horse down is to have too strong a hand on its reins. This used to be the right approach in business—back when the level-one ideal of a top-down, tightly controlled workplace was more appropriate. Management used to be described as controlling people and their work. And the expression "who's in control here" still refers to the manager in charge. But there has been a gradual shift in thinking about the manager's role. Where it used to be considered best to control your employees, now the ideal is to manage by helping your employees control their own work.

Getting Out of the Way: Motivating by Giving Control

As a manager, you certainly need to control the work to the extent needed to ensure that the right work is done well. That's your responsibility—and it's a big one. You need to understand the big picture of what needs to be done and why, and you need to make sure that macro goals are broken down into appropriate micro-level goals and tasks—and that your people understand and do these tasks well. Such tools as plans, schedules, lists, and feedback systems all help you maintain this necessary level of management control.

But whereas the old-style manager might have tried also to control the details of what people did, and when and how they did it, the modern manager tries to push more of these details out into the hands (and minds) of his employees. The ideal is to achieve central control over the work by having individual employees exercise a high degree of self-control over their own work.

Why this switch? Why should you try to give employees more autonomy over their work, and how can that help you as a manager do a better job of controlling your results?

The reason has to do with the rationale for focusing on intrinsic motivation and trying to stimulate initiative and commitment in your people. If you think back to the exercises in Chapter 1, you may remember listing words to describe the ideal employee. Characteristics like problem-solving, taking initiative, being enthusiastic, and being creative are associated with intrinsic motivation—and also with the feeling that you are in control of the situation. And when people feel like they lack personal control, they lose initiative, and their intrinsic motivation evaporates.

Autonomy (or personal control over one's situation) is a very important driver of the level of intrinsic motivation in your employees. If you do everything else right, but don't give employees much control, they will slip off the motivation path and adopt a negative view of their work. Lack of control is therefore a potential contaminant that you want to make sure does not get into your workplace.

The Helplessness Problem
You may have heard of learned helplessness. It's a relatively new discovery in psychology, and it occurs when someone feels like they can't control the outcomes and are stuck and helpless to fix things. If you are not able to affect outcomes directly, you can slip into a frame of mind where you just don't care and stop trying to make a difference. You may even get depressed. You certainly won't be motivated.

According to the authors of a leading book on the subject, "Control is such an important psychological process that it affects our very brain chemistry."[1] So control has emerged in recent years as an important factor in explaining whether people take initiative and are motivated or not.

And among employees who lack motivation, it is pretty common to find that they also feel their managers give them little or no control. They can't decide where they work, how they decorate the office, with whom they work, when they work, what they do, and when and how they do it.

As a manager, you need to be sensitive to the many little ways in which you can *give control* of working conditions, the work environment, and the ways in which work is done. There is much that you can do that has great symbolic value and imparts a real sense of control, but that doesn't go so far as to put your results at risk. Let people decorate or rearrange their work spaces. When assembling project groups or teams, select one or two core people and let them pick the rest. Even when you have to set policy or announce a decision, you can increase people's sense of control by giving them choices instead of a single option. And using the motivational communication techniques from Chapter 4 can help increase self-control for your people by encouraging them to participate in all decisions affecting their work.

Exercise 8-1. What did YOU wish you could control?

Whenever we think back to old jobs, there are always things that we wished we could have had more control over. Maybe the company had a rigid policy on what we could wear or what pictures we could display. Or maybe the boss didn't allow us to bend a rule now and then when we thought it necessary in order to satisfy an upset customer. Perhaps it was the way that a manager controlled the conversation in meetings, keeping us from exploring ideas because the agenda had to be followed religiously. Or maybe it was the lack of flextime, or the way the company didn't allow us to bring in our own coffee maker. When we stop to think about it, there are many such control issues that have bothered each and every one of us at some time in the past. Take a moment now to list some of the things you wished you could have had more control over in past jobs:

1.

2.

3.

4.

5.

6.

It takes some effort to get your head into this exercise and come up with a good list. Now that you've done it, you may find it easier to see how your employees have control issues too. When possible, loosen the controls that bug them. Each time you do, you are investing in their intrinsic motivation. (And if you can't, explain why—so they have that all-important "line of sight" from what they have to do to the broader purpose for it.)

How Controlling Are You?

Because our society has a long tradition of controlling styles of management (and controlling styles of teaching and parenting too), most of us have controlling habits that tend to shape our management style without our realizing it. So as you work on becoming a manager who gives the gift of control instead of taking it, you may find it helpful to test your habits and find out whether they are working against you. To change any habit, you have to start by making yourself fully aware of it after all.

Here is an interesting exercise that helps you be more aware of any control habits you may have.

Exercise 8-2. Self-evaluation of controlling management behaviors.

To find out how controlling your management habits are, simply read each of the following statements and decide how well they fit you. Use this scale:

1 = strongly disagree
2 = disagree
3 = undecided
4 = agree
5 = strongly agree

As a manager:

1 2 3 4 5   I need to know what my employees are doing all the time.

1 2 3 4 5   I tell people to do their work the way I would do it.

1 2 3 4 5   I control the agenda for all my staff meetings.

1 2 3 4 5   I usually control the flow of information in my group.

1 2 3 4 5   I prefer to manage details.

1 2 3 4 5   I prepare detailed plans of action for my people to follow.

1 2 3 4 5   I don't like employees to personalize their work spaces.

1 2 3 4 5   I don't like employees to improvise instead of following policies and procedures.

1 2 3 4 5   I expect employees to ask me what to do whenever a problem arises.

1 2 3 4 5   I don't feel comfortable asking employees what they think.

1 2 3 4 5   I don't feel comfortable leaving employees alone.

1 2 3 4 5   I get upset when employees don't do things my way.

Now total your scores to find out what they add up to. There are twelve scores, each ranging from a low of 1 to a high of 5, so the range for the total is from 12 to 60. Dividing this range into thirds, we can say that any score in the bottom third of the range (28 or lower) is low on the controlling scale. Any score from 29 to 44 is medium and indicates a number of controlling habits that need to be watched and reduced. And any score of 45 or higher on the control scale indicates a need to reduce controlling behaviors significantly.

12–28   Low
29–44   Medium
45–60   High

Exploring Your Role Models

Another exercise that is sometimes helpful is to think of managers you have worked for or with, who were very controlling, and ones who were the opposite—who gave their people lots of opportunities for self-control. Come up with an example of each—one person who represents controlling management and another who is the opposite. Now stop and think about the ways they differed. What were the biggest differences between them? This exercise helps personalize the issue of control by anchoring it in some examples and behaviors with which you are particularly familiar.

Micro-Planning?

Also think about the differences between controlling and noncontrolling approaches to planning. If you had to write a plan for your department, team, or business, how would a controlling approach differ from a noncontrolling approach? Again, this is an interesting exercise that may help you come up with insights you can apply to managing your own behavior. For example, if you have to plan something, are you going to include your employees in the process—and if so, to what extent and how? And once the plan is written, will you insist that it be followed to the letter, or will you write a looser plan that leaves room for learning and improvement upon initial ideas?

You Can't Raise Their Motivation Higher than Your Own

This chapter focuses on factors that can sabotage your efforts to boost employee motivation. Control is certainly an important example, and when employees feel like they lack personal control over their work and work environment, they lose motivation and their performances suffer. But there are other factors that can also spoil employee attitudes and block the success of your motivational management initiatives. A common one is low personal motivation. If you are not feeling very good about your *own* work, it is going to be hard to get other people motivated.

A CASE IN POINT

Imagine that you supervise Joan, the employee we've discussed throughout this book. It's been a busy week, and you have hardly had a chance to talk to her. You know she is busy with several reports right now, but your own work is overwhelming you, and you haven't had the time to check on Joan's progress. Besides, you are hesitant to talk to your employees too much right now because everyone is so discouraged by the most recent round of layoffs. You know they'll just start complaining if you give them the opening, and you don't feel up to listening to them vent. You have problems of your own to worry about.

On Wednesday afternoon, you learn that another report has to be prepared in a hurry for delivery this Friday. You hate to assign even more work to Joan, but what choice do you have? Feeling a bit embarrassed, you drop the file on her desk and mumble something about how the report needs to be done by Friday. Then you go back to your office, close the door, and stare at the huge pile of work in your own in-box.

You have to admit you are feeling discouraged and aren't sure how you'll handle your own workload. In your current frame of mind, it is hard to imagine giving Joan much help or encouragement. You don't have much motivation to share right now. In fact, you feel so low you decide to just go home early and put off figuring out what to do until tomorrow. You hope Joan doesn't notice as you slip out the back door.

Every manager has down periods like the one described in this scenario. There are times when the work can seem overwhelming or you can feel like you aren't making much progress. You may have days (or even weeks) where you feel depressed and unable to control your own fate. If this happens, recognize that your mood is negative rather than positive—and that it is going to keep you from stimulating positive feelings in your employees. In fact, the manager's mood is especially catching. If you feel down, you can easily spread your negative attitude to your employees.

Take a moment to imagine how your mood might affect Joan in the above scenario. If you were Joan, and your manager behaved the way you did, you probably wouldn't feel very good either. In fact, in the earlier chapters we looked at this same story from Joan's point of view, and from there it looked like Joan's manager was inconsiderate and unsupportive and did not know how to be a motivational manager. That is the employee's view, but the manager's view may be quite different from what the employee sees. A manager who is caught up in stressful or overwhelming workloads and is feeling discouraged is not able to provide motivational management. And although he may appear to be inconsiderate and insensitive to the employees, it may simply be that he has too much on his mind to be able to fill the motivational management role at the moment.

So, when you are not feeling positive and highly motivated yourself, you need to:

1. Isolate yourself emotionally from your employees to avoid bringing them down.

2. Work on your own motivation before you work on theirs.

This is a very important principle and practice, one that will keep you from accidentally spoiling employee attitudes. You can't expect to manage other people's emotions if you cannot manage your own. So you have to be prepared to work on your own feelings and move yourself into an active, positive perspective whenever you slip out of it.

How can you do this? How can you boost your own motivation so that you are emotionally prepared to motivate others?

For starters, you need to think about what things tend to make you feel positive and good about your work. Take a moment to do the following exercise.

Exercise 8-3. What makes ME feel motivated?

Everyone experiences a range of motivational feelings, from low to high. Think about times when you feel especially motivated and have energy and enthusiasm to spare. What factors help you feel that way? When do those feelings occur? To help identify things that make you feel motivated, stop and ask yourself the following questions:

1. What activities make you feel powerful, able, in charge, capable?
2. What activities make you feel relaxed, calm, happy, content?
3. What activities make you feel more in control of your schedule or workload?
4. What activities remind you of your past successes and make you feel confident in your ability to achieve greater successes in the future?
5. What person or people tend to make you feel up and positive when you spend time with them?
6. What activities make you feel strong and healthy?

This exercise breaks down the question of what makes you motivated into six separate, smaller questions to help make it easy to answer. In answering them, don't feel you have to fill in every one. Different people turn their moods around in different ways. However, do be careful not to list things that give you a false feeling of motivation—one that does not last and leaves you feeling worse later on.

For example, think about the difference between eating a big piece of cake and a big serving of some healthy main-course food. The sweet dessert will make you feel good for a little while—perhaps only for as long as it takes to eat it. The more nutritious food may not make you feel as good right away, but over time it will boost your energy and make you feel stronger and more healthy. So as you read your list and look for things you can do to manage your own motivation, *favor those motivators that have the most lasting impact.* Going for a walk or jog, for example, is far more effective at boosting one's motivation than having an alcoholic drink.

Use the list you compiled in Exercise 8-3 when you feel down and, if at all possible, before you interact with your employees. Also stop and examine your own work to make sure you have clear goals—and that you know how your work relates to those goals and how to do your work well. If you are struggling with meaningless or overly challenging work or lack clear goals, you too will lose motivation, just like your employees do. You may need to stop and apply the methods from earlier chapters to your own work before you have the motivation to apply them well to others' work.

Oh, by the way, once you compile a list of the things you do to boost your own motivation, you might want to take a critical look at that list. Are too many of the activities short-term in their effect? Are there not enough activities? You can always try something new and add to the list. And as you make progress on your ability to self-manage your work-related mood, you will find it easier and easier to manage others positively and productively too.

Eliminating Unfairness

Another common contaminant is unfairness. As a manager, you probably never intend to treat employees unfairly, so you wouldn't expect them to feel that you are unfair. But in truth, many employees feel like they are being treated unfairly. Perhaps they have been treated unfairly in the past, and that makes them a bit suspicious and quick to assume they are being treated unfairly now. Or maybe there are unfair policies in the organization that affect how employees feel, even if you yourself are a fair manager.

So it is important to check for the perception of unfairness and keep an eye out for this potentially damaging negative emotion. If you detect it, stop and talk it through and, if necessary, take some simple steps to make people feel better. For example, imagine that Joan says to you, "But it's not fair that I always have to pick up the slack and do the extra reports." Her feeling that she is getting an unfair share of the work is important because it can spoil her motivation in a hurry. What should you do?

First, you need to think about what she said and see if she is correct. Perhaps there are others who could do just as good a job on the report you need to get done—others who have not had to do as much extra work as Joan. If so, then simply thank her for pointing this out and reassign the task. But in many cases, it's not that simple. Often you have little choice. If so, then explain why.

If Joan understands your reasons, it will be a great antidote to her feeling of unfairness. If Joan is the only available employee who can do the report well and the report has to get done right away, well, then you can simply explain that to her. Then of course you need to thank her and tell her you are sorry she has to do extra work. Acknowledge the unfairness and let her know you appreciate and sympathize with her. Finally, in the future, try to find ways around loading Joan up with too much work. A short-term unfairness for a good cause is not going to be a problem, but if you don't do something to make Joan's workload more reasonable in the long term, it will eventually prove damaging.

So, to summarize, the process for handling an employee's feeling of unfairness is:

1. See if they are right—and if so, adjust accordingly!

2. Give them clear information so they understand the situation.

3. If the information truly does indicate an unfairness and there is nothing to be done about it in the short term, offer sincere sympathy and appreciation for their extra effort or inconvenience.

4. Work on leveling things out to eliminate the unfairness in the longer term.

Also note that there are some kinds of unfair treatment that are illegal as well as unfair. Illegalities should never be tolerated, even in the short term. For example, nobody should be treated unfairly (skipped for a promotion, not hired for a job, harassed, etc.) because of age, gender, religion, race, disability, or national origin. If you become aware of any discrimination like this or anyone complains about it, take immediate *action*. Hopefully you have a company lawyer or human resource department that can help you figure out what to do to remedy the situation. Seek expert help at once (and in the meantime, do whatever seems reasonable and sensitive in terms of protecting your employees from further injury).

These sorts of concerns and complaints are serious stuff and may cost you and your firm a lot in legal expenses and ongoing trouble if you don't take care of them right away. And they can do a great deal to damage employee motivation and hurt performance, not just among those directly concerned but often throughout the entire work group.

Untangling Compensation from Motivation

If employees feel unfairly compensated, they will not be positive about their work, and you will have no luck getting them motivated. Sometimes employees will be perfectly content with their level of compensation until something happens to make them question it. For instance, perhaps a recruiter calls and tells them about a similar position at another company where their compensation would be substantially higher. This could introduce a nagging suspicion that they are being underpaid and taken advantage of—which could be the end of their enthusiasm for their job. To avoid such problems, I recommend that employees be paid at or above the average for their types of jobs in the geographic area where they work. Then you can feel confident that they are indeed being paid fairly—and you can tell them that your policy is to do so.

There are plenty of ways to find out what typical salaries are. If you work in a larger company, your HR Department already collects such information and can share it with you (they probably already have normalized salaries, and if you learn the details you will be able to put any rumors to rest with authority). If you work in a small business, you may need to surf the Web or contact a reference librarian or talk to a recruiter or check want ads in the newspaper to compile a relevant salary survey. If you learn that your people are earning roughly what they are worth in the job market right now, then you can simply let them know you think it is important that they be paid fairly, and that you are keeping an eye on the market and will do your best to make sure they continue to be. That should help to eliminate their concerns.

However, if you find that your people are indeed underpaid,

well, at least you know you have a problem and you know what it is. As a result, you should expect employee concerns about compensation to be a drag on motivation until you or your employer can correct the situation. Sometimes it is easy to fix—a small adjustment here and there. In other circumstances it can be more of a problem. A company that is losing money or making very little profit may not be able to raise salaries or offer more competitive benefits in the short term. In such cases the best policy is honesty. Let the employee(s) know that you know about the problem and that you do view it as a problem you want to solve when you can. Then make it clear that you hope that if everyone tries hard, your firm will be able to turn things around, and everyone will benefit in the long run. If the employees believe in the potential of the company, they will often stay and fight it out—especially if they know their employers want to pay them fairly and expect to do so as soon as possible.

But two cautions are in order. First, if you do not have full authority to negotiate compensation, better to check with those who do before making any commitments or even suggestions about future increases. You don't want to raise expectations unrealistically. Second, there are protocols and legal issues involved in the compensation area that aren't being covered in this book, so make sure you have good advice or involve those within your firm who have the relevant expertise before discussing compensation policies with your employees.

Eliminating Secrets: The Need for Open-Book Communications

Feelings of unfairness and concerns about unjust treatment always arise when there are secrets. And most of them evaporate when information is shared. So the simplest way to avoid the contaminating effects of unfairness is to open the books as much as possible to employees. Let them know what is going on and how the business is doing. Let them know what the major issues and problems are. Tell them about upcoming executive meetings and what major decisions are going to be discussed so they won't be unpleasantly surprised by a change of plan.

Most of what companies keep secret from their employees is actually not at all sensitive. No harm will come from sharing it. And a great deal of good may come from sharing the information since that is such a good way to keep secrets from contaminating employee motivation.

Basically, you should only keep information from your employees when there is a clear, compelling reason to do so.

Managing Conflicts Productively

Conflicts and disagreements are another common contaminant of positive work attitudes. If your employees are in conflicts that don't get resolved well, then you can expect their motivation to fall. Conflicts can raise stress levels and leave people feeling hurt and upset. Even silly conflicts that don't seem important to you can feel important to your employees. As a manager, you need to be aware of conflicts, and you need to take an interest in seeing them resolved well.

That said, you also need to stay on the sidelines in conflicts. You don't want to play referee. That's a variation on stop-light management, and it does not encourage employees to take responsibility for their own behavior. In addition, when managers try to step onto the field and set the ground rules for conflicts, the employees often try to draw them into playing for one side or the other—and that you definitely want to avoid. There is usually no benefit in your getting drawn into your employees' conflicts.

So how can you help your people manage their own conflicts productively? You might want to actually get some training in conflict management, because there are a great many skills you could learn and use as a manager. But there are also some simple things you can do. You can:

> ▶ *Ask lots of questions.* Good conflict behavior explores the other party's situation and tries to understand why they feel as they do. If you set the tone by asking questions that help

raise underlying issues and concerns, you will increase the use of this healthy conflict-management technique in your employees too.

▶ *Listen.* Listening skills are the most powerful tool for resolving conflicts productively. Passive listening involves simply being open and taking in what they say. Active listening seeks to clarify and verify what you hear with questions that reflect back what you think they are saying and ask them if you are hearing it right.

▶ *Insist on creative problem-solving.* If the conflict is important, then ask for and insist upon clever, creative solutions to it. Push your people to come up with good solutions, not just any old solution that sweeps the conflict under the rug quickly but fails to resolve it well.

If you simply apply these three strategies when dealing with employee conflicts, you will do much to raise the level of conflict management in your work group—and you will thereby avoid many of the negative effects that conflict can have on employee motivation.

Avoid Communicating in Anger

One note of caution is in order, however. When people are angry, they cannot use these strategies effectively. Anger keeps us from communicating well. I was thinking about this the other day when I was exercising in San Francisco's Golden Gate Park. I like to go to a big oval track at the old Polo Grounds there and roller-skate. As I was tearing along, a large dog rushed toward me, snarling and snapping at my legs. I barely managed to fend it off and stop without falling, and was greatly relieved to find myself on the side of the track a few seconds later, still standing and in one piece. I was also madder than a hornet, and called out loudly to the owners of the dog to get it under control. Then one of them (the man of the couple of course—we guys tend to do this kind of thing, right?) came running full tilt toward me, shouting at the top of his voice, "I SAID we're SORRY!" over and over, until he was inches from me, his eyes bugging out, screaming his message in my face along with a fair amount of saliva in spray form. If I hadn't departed as quickly as I could, I think he would have showed me just how sorry he felt by biting my leg himself.

Now, was this conflict situation going to be resolved using any of the three techniques I described above? Certainly not. We weren't really communicating. My attacker probably does not even remember exactly what he said or did. His verbal message was so contradictory to his feelings and actions that it is a perfect illustration of the failure of communications when anger intrudes. This was not a good moment to try to communicate with him, to say the least. Almost anything I could have said or done right then would have escalated the conflict.

In situations like these where anger seems to be ascendant, the only good option is separation. Everyone involved in the conflict needs to be separated and given time to cool down and return to "their right mind," as the old-but-true expression puts it. So please keep in mind the destructive power of anger, and practice avoidance whenever it gets in the way. Bide your time and wait until you can create a situation in which calm communication is at least possible. Then you can try to use good communication skills to defuse conflict—so as to keep it from contaminating your positive, productive workplace.

(I need to add a note concerning violent behavior in the workplace. Verbal and/or physical abuse is never appropriate, and should be reported immediately. If your workplace does not already have procedures for responding to abusive behavior and for trying to prevent potential violence and injuries, please get to work on this. Although rare on a per-capita basis, violence does occur regularly in workplaces, so it is a serious concern for all managers. It is not within the scope of this book, but should be within the scope of management.)

Summary

Once again we've covered quite a range of subjects in a single chapter, so let's revisit them briefly and integrate them into the big-picture goal of eliminating as many motivation-killers as possible.

All your efforts to build initiative and positive work attitudes can be spoiled if employees feel they lack control in their work. Also, your own level of motivation affects theirs, so if you are demotivated, this can spoil their attitudes. Employees also lose motivation when they feel they are being treated unfairly, or when workplace conflicts disrupt them and they are not able to resolve the conflicts productively and well. As a manager you need to be on guard for these possible contaminants and take appropriate steps to deal with them.

There are many ways that you can give employees more choices and options and let them have more control over their own work and working conditions once you stop to think about it. And when you examine your management style, you may find ways in which you tend to be a controlling manager without meaning to.

Also, it is a good idea to watch your own mood and catch yourself when your motivation is low. That's not a good time to try to lead your employees. Instead, work on turning your own attitude around so that you will once again have enthusiasm to share with your people.

When employees feel they are receiving unfair treatment, their motivation tends to fall, so it is important to keep an eye out for this problem and intervene when you detect it. Good communications with your employees and a sincere effort to make things as fair as is reasonably possible will prevent the issue from spoiling employee motivation in your group.

When conflicts upset the mood in your group of employees, you need to encourage productive resolution by demonstrating the power of good conflict management techniques. For example, listening, asking questions to explore each party's underlying interests, and striving to find creative, nonobvious solutions are important skills that you can share with your employees. Conflicts are a natural part of working life, but they should not be covered up, nor should they be allowed to spiral out of control. By encouraging conflicts to be worked on in the open, you can prevent them from spoiling motivation in your group.

Notes

1. Christopher Peterson, Martin E. Seligman, and Steven F. Maier, *Learned Helplessness* (New York: Oxford University Press, 1993).

Transforming Negative Attitudes

Think you can, think you can't;
either way, you'll be right.

—Henry Ford

How often do our employees think they can, and how often do they think they can't? If negative, defeatist attitudes do indeed get in the way of successful performances, then this is something we definitely want to manage.

It is fascinating how every successful executive or entrepreneur—or really, anyone who has succeeded to a high degree in any field of endeavor—seems to have a remarkably positive attitude. The American industrialist Henry J. Kaiser is quoted as having said that "problems are only opportunities in work clothes." Vincent van Gogh, who many believe to be one of the greatest painters of all time but whose work was unrecognized during his lifetime, said that "great things are not something accidental, but must certainly be willed." And Helen Keller argued that "no pessimist ever discovered the secrets of the stars, or sailed to an uncharted land, or opened a new heaven to the human spirit."

I'm sure she is right, but on the other hand, I am also pretty sure that the typical workforce has a goodly share of pessimists in it. And they are not bashful about sharing their negative attitudes. Let's look at a typical example.

Your staff meeting is just ending and some of the employees are chatting as they collect their notes and prepare to go back to work. You can't help overhearing their conversations, and you wonder about the attitudes they seem to reflect.

One employee says to another, "You just can't win with the HR department. They always find some way to make it tough to collect on your travel expense claims." The companion says, "Oh, I didn't know that. I haven't had to file any claims since I came here."

You shake your head and turn away, sorry to hear an older employee passing on a negative attitude to one of your new hires, but figuring it is really none of your business. You know from your own experience that filing claims can be complicated, but that the HR department does not want to make it tougher than it has to be. In truth, difficulties generally arise because employees don't provide full information or fail to file for reimbursement in a timely manner, yet you know frustrations often arise and you aren't surprised to hear someone blaming the company for their problems. Still, what can you do? It's a private conversation and none of your business. Or is it?

Why Negative Talk Matters

Negative talk between employees *is* your business as a manager, because it damages work motivation and contaminates attitudes, spreading a negative view of the workplace that can undo all your good efforts to build employee motivation.

Specifically, the negative-speaking employee in the case above is feeling victimized and is communicating this victim role to others. That's a negative attitude you don't want spreading, as it quickly saps employees' energy and initiative.

In addition, the employee's offhand comments about her expenses reflect a conflict-oriented approach. She assumes she is in conflict with her company's HR department and portrays it as an us-against-them struggle to her coworker, thereby spreading a negative attitude to him.

There may well be difficulties and complex issues associated with expense claims—especially if documentation is lacking—but by assuming the HR department is on one side of a battle and she is on the other, this employee takes a conflict-oriented approach that could easily spill over to other relationships at work. A positive attitude toward the same situation might lead her to stop by and ask for help in a friendly manner, and that might get her much better results than griping. But her conflict-oriented approach not only gets in the way of her seeking help and doing productive problem-solving in this situation, it *also spreads an uncooperative spirit to other situations and other people in the workplace.*

Notice also that this employee's complaint to her coworker reflects a fundamental acceptance of what she sees as a negative *status quo*. She says "you can't win" and that "they always . . ." This sense that the situation is irrevocably bad and cannot be improved is highly negative. It may spread and lead others to accept frustrations blindly rather than try to improve them. So there are many subtle ways in which that negative conversation can sap energy, hurt motivation, and destroy enthusiasm, willingness, and initiative.

Negative Attitudes Are Catching (But So Are Positive Ones!)

Negative attitudes are never confined to one subject. They always spill over from one area to another and so can quickly destroy motivation and hurt performance. Someone who voices a feeling of helplessness and victimization about a minor, personal situation can and will spread that sense of helplessness and victimization to other people and situations, some of which will be important to the business you manage.

Because attitudes are catching, it is important to transform negative attitudes to positive ones and to try to spread positive attitudes rather than allowing negative ones to spread uncontrolled. As a manager, you can tap into your awareness of negative talk and you can use simple conversational devices to transform negative talk to positive talk. In fact, the open questioning techniques you learned in Chapter 4 are a good general antidote to negative talk, and we will supplement them with some specific antidotes in this chapter.

Employees (and managers) often engage in attitude talk, or conversations that communicate their basic attitudes and feelings. Especially when we feel frustrated, it is natural to share our negative feelings in our talk with others. Some experts compare this to emptying our own buckets of emotions into other people's. It feels good to vent and get some of those negative feelings out in the open. But it doesn't do any good to pour them into someone else's bucket. Yet that's what negative talk tends to do.

When Style of Talk Is More Important than Substance

We usually pay more attention to *what* we say than *how* we say it. But to work on making talk more positive, you need to tune your ear to how people talk. You need to recognize that the way you say something can and often does determine what you say—and how you feel and act. This is especially true when it comes to negative talk, the conversations (live or by e-mail or phone) that arise out of an urge to unload frustration, anger, or other negative emotions.

Our style of talk shapes the content and sometimes even *becomes* the message. When someone allows negative ways of thinking and speaking to shape their conversation, they will express narrow, pessimistic, limiting viewpoints. Their style of talk will allow negative attitudes to infect their thinking. And their negative talking style also spreads that negative viewpoint to others.

To counter the hidden dangers of negative speaking patterns, it helps to recognize five closely related types of "attitude talk." Each type can be negative *or* positive. If you learn to recognize negative forms of attitude talk and rephrase them into positive forms, you will find that you can produce positive, can-do attitudes in yourself and others in five simple ways, as the next section explores.

Transforming a Negative into a Positive

ID badges displayed on chains around the neck are increasingly common in workplaces as security-conscious managers realize that access should be controlled. But when everyone has to display a standardized, impersonal security ID, it can, well, depersonalize things. Is this a negative, something to bring folks down, something to complain about at the water cooler? Depends on how you look at it.

Crystal Chow, a *San Jose Mercury News* reporter, noticed a trend among Silicon Valley businesses toward having some fun with IDs. All sorts of individual statements are beginning to appear on or in place of those ID chains. She tracked down a millefiori bead maker, Kim Korringa of Mountain View, who has made a number of entertaining and unique ID necklaces for clients.

And she also visited with Paula Stout, head of corporate communications at the Palo Alto office of German software company SAP, where individual expression via IDs is rampant. According to Stout, in her office the ID lanyard has become "a place for self-expression." People decorate them with pins, flags, and, "at Christmas someone even decorated it with blinking lights." Others carry "portable offices" on theirs, with things like cell-phone ear jacks, pens, and keys along with their IDs.[1]

How important is it to find vehicles for self-expression in the workplace—especially when they are countering a potentially depersonalizing and controlling element like an ID badge? Well, you can probably guess how I'd answer that question from the way I asked it! But here are two questions you can answer on your own:

▶ What things are currently sending a depersonalizing or other potentially negative message to your employees?

▶ Can you think of ways to seed some creative practices to counter that effect?

How Common Is Negative Talk?[2]

There are probably as many types of negative talk as there are pessimists—people are remarkably creative when it comes to finding ways to say the sky is falling! But it is helpful to recognize at least five common forms of negative talk that are heard all too frequently in businesses and workplaces today. Exhibit 9-1 describes them, and we'll take a closer look at each one later in this chapter. But first, let's find out how common these various forms of negative talk are in your workplace.

Negative Talk Assessment

Exercise 9-1 is based on an assessment tool we often use in workshops. It gives you an indication of how much negative talk there is in your workplace.

EXHIBIT 9-1. Types of negative talk. ————————————————

1. Accepting vs. Rejecting
Accepting instead of rejecting limits and boundaries.

2. Narrowing vs. Expanding
Allowing yourself to be mentally "trapped" or limited by preconceived notions, instead of creating more choices and options.

3. Victimized vs. In Charge
Feeling victimized instead of feeling in charge of the events in your life.

4. Blaming vs. Understanding
Judging or blaming yourself or others, instead of seeking a broader understanding that allows you to avoid such problems in the future.

5. Conflicting vs. Cooperating
Reacting defensively in conflicts instead of reaching out to find common ground and develop ways to meet everyone's needs.

————————————————————————————————————

Exercise 9-1. Negative talk assessment (short version).

Read the following statements and classify each based on whether you hear such statements *never, rarely, sometimes,* or *often* in your workplace. At the end, add up the totals in each of the four answer columns and see which one is the highest. This gives you an idea of how negative or positive the talk is right now. "Sometimes" and "Often" answers indicate a negative talk problem. If you apply the methods in this chapter, you should be able to move your score more toward "Rarely" or "Never."

Negative Statements	How often do you hear statements like the examples in your workplace? *Circle* one of the options.

1. *Accepting Limits*	Never Rarely Sometimes Often

Examples:
You can't do that.
If only . . .
I'm stuck.
I don't know how.
It's not my job.
It's out of my hands.
You've got to follow the program.

2. *Narrowing Options*	Never Rarely Sometimes Often

Examples:
We've only got two options and neither is appealing.
There's no way out.
We are out of time.
I'm sure I am right.
It's my way or the highway.
But the policy is to . . .
This is how we always do it.

3. *Feeling Victimized by Events*	Never Rarely Sometimes Often

Examples:
Why do bad things always happen to me?
I got bad news today.

I can't help it.
You sure are lucky.
They won't let us do that anymore.
You really messed me up.
That's not our responsibility.
That's not my department.
There's nothing *I* can do.

4. *Blaming Fate or Others*	Never	Rarely	Sometimes	Often

Examples:
You're responsible for this, aren't you?
He should have known better.
Who's responsible for this mistake?
Why did you do it that way?
Didn't you know that . . . ?
That was stupid.
I'd like to know who's responsible.

5. *Encouraging Conflicts*	Never	Rarely	Sometimes	Often

Examples:
It's my turn.
If you don't _____, I'll _____.
You're not listening!
_____ really ticks me off.
I'll only do this if you do that.
I've got plenty of problems of my own.
I don't want to talk to _____.
I don't care what he thinks.

Totals. Count the number of answers in each of the categories for an overall indication of how frequent negative talk is in your workplace.	Never	Rarely	Sometimes	Often

Did you find that some of the negative talk patterns in Exercise 9-1 occur in your workplace? Most people do, because they are quite common among employees in almost all workplaces. As a manager, you can think of your job in part as working on reducing the frequency of such negative talk, since this will help boost motivation and improve employee performances. In the following sections of this chapter we'll take a close look at all five types of negative talk and practice transforming them into more positive versions.

1. Accepting vs. Rejecting

This kind of negative talk is all about how we unconsciously accept limits and boundaries. It is countered by talking about ways to reject boundaries by getting around them or eliminating them entirely.

A limit can be anything that holds us back—whether we notice it or not. When you encounter limitations, do they make you feel like finding a way around them, or do they make you feel like giving up? Depends on how you think—and talk—about the limit, as these two examples illustrate:

▶ *Negative Example*: "There's no way to get this mailing out on time."

▶ *Positive Example*: "There must be some way to get this mailing out on time."

A CASE IN POINT

Imagine one of your employees is faced with a situation in which he is expected to make a number of photocopies of a lengthy report and send them out to a list of people in the overnight mail. There is only half an hour until the overnight packages are picked up for the day at the drop box in your company's lobby. The photocopy machine breaks down, and a few quick calls reveal that none of the other machines in the building are working correctly right now either. What does the employee do?

Ideally, as this employee's manager you want him to take initiative to find a solution to the problem. You can imagine many possible ways to overcome the barriers of time and broken equipment and get the job done.

▶ Maybe he should rush out to a copy shop or ask to use the equipment in a neighboring company's offices.

▶ Maybe the document could be scanned and printed out on a plain-paper fax machine or computer.

▶ Maybe it is on disk and can simply be printed out multiple times on a laser printer.

▶ Maybe the recipients wouldn't mind getting an e-mail version of it and printing it themselves.

▶ And perhaps there is a drop-box or pickup point for overnight delivery service that has a later pickup time than the one in the lobby of your building.

But for the employee to even think of exploring such options, he must first take a positive approach. He won't if he is accustomed to hearing and using negative talk. Instead he'll say something like, "That report can't go out today, all the copy machines are broken and it's too late in the day. It'll have to wait until tomorrow." In fact, negative talk like that is common in workplaces unless the manager creates the expectation that employees will think and talk positively about such problems.

That's why you always want to restate negative talk about barriers and limits. As a manager you need to model a different kind of attitude in your talk so that it will come to mind when employees are in a situation like this. You want the employee's default reaction to be to say to himself or to others, "Hey, I've got a problem getting this report out. I wonder how many ways I can think of to overcome this problem and accomplish my goal?"

To make sure the employee will respond in that manner with

a positive effort to overcome the barrier, you need to put in place positive talk about barriers and limits in general. Whenever you hear people talking about limits in a negative, *can't do* way, you need to politely, even humorously, rephrase their talk into a positive *can do* form.

For instance, imagine again that you overhear an employee grumbling about how impossible it is to get some expense claim processed properly. Although you don't have direct management responsibility for that employee's reimbursements, you do have an active interest in rephrasing negative talk. And so you might say something like, "Sorry to hear that, I know it can be frustrating. Can you think of ways of getting around the problem you're having?"

When you challenge yourself to think of positive talk to replace negative talk, at first it can seem difficult. But with a little practice it gets easy to come up with many possible statements or questions that might do the trick. For example, again in the situation where you hear an employee complain about expense claims, you might ask any number of variants that are positive and action-oriented, such as one of the following:

> ► "I think some of the employees seem to know how to work the system so as to get their claims handled more easily. I wonder how they do it."

> ► "It would be great if somebody did something about that problem. Have you considered stopping by the HR department and chatting with them about it? They might have some ideas or information you could use to simplify the process."

> ► "I gather that most claims go through okay, but some of them get held up, which makes me wonder why. Do you have any idea what issues typically cause the trouble? Maybe if we found out it would be possible to avoid holdups in the future."

The point of exploring many positive alternatives is that positive thinking is *creative*. It turns lemons into lemonade. Or lemon bars. Or lemon scones. Or lemon wedges to use in your tea. Or lemon oil for polishing furniture. Or anything productive and positive—it hardly matters what as long as you take a creative attitude and voice thoughts that generate options instead of encouraging employees to give up and accept limitations.

Exercise 9-2. Transforming negative talk with positive questions.

When an employee says, "I can't figure out how the new software works," you could encourage them to think more positively by asking them some questions. Write down two or more questions:

Sample Solutions

"Do you know anyone you can ask?"

"Have you taken the tutorial?"

"Is the manual useful?"

"Is it similar to any software you know?"

"How have you learned other software in the past?"

"What would you need to do to learn it?"

"You know how to do some things on it already, right? How did you learn them and can you use the same approach to learn more?"

2. Narrowing vs. Expanding

Narrowing is when you talk about a problem as if there is only one or a few ways to approach it. Saying "Fred is terribly forgetful, I guess I'm going to have to stop giving him any important responsibilities" is a narrowing statement that blinds you to the possibilities of doing something about his forgetfulness. Narrowing negative talk leads us to feel mentally "trapped" or limited by preconceived notions, instead of taking the initiative to create more choices and options.

Have you ever done brainstorming? The majority of people have been exposed to this classic idea-generating technique at some point in school or in a training program at work. It involves generating lots and lots of unfiltered ideas, anything that pops into your mind in association with a particular problem or other topic. It is one way to open up your thinking and try to surface new approaches, and it can be very effective. Yet less than 1 percent of people report having used brainstorming in the last month in their work.* This reflects the fact that we seldom stop to generate creative alternatives at work.

Creative behavior is not traditionally part of the workplace culture in most organizations. But to overcome negative talk you often need to shift the conversation to a discussion of creative alternatives. That helps employees escape from corners their thinking has backed them into.

For example, imagine that you hear a fellow manager complaining about an employee who is not performing well. The manager is frustrated and feels the employee is not trying to improve. The manager says to you, "I don't know what to do. I can either fire her or overlook her poor performance, and I don't really want to do either."

If you allow this statement to limit the options to just the two

* In my talks and trainings I often ask audiences of employees or managers whether they know how to do brainstorming, and most of them say yes. Then I ask them whether they have used the technique recently. Hardly any have.

presented—firing her or ignoring the problem—then you know the manager will not resolve the problem productively. And you know that negative talk and negative thinking will have scored another victory and will be in danger of spreading. So you could counter with a positive statement designed to help your fellow manager focus on expanding the possible options. You might say something as simple as, "Since you don't like either of those options, can you come up with some new options to consider?"

Often a little nudge in the positive direction is all it takes to get people out of a negative rut. The manager might respond to your positive talk by saying something like, "You're right. I need to come up with some better options for dealing with her. Hmm. How about giving her daily written feedback, or I could pair her with a 'mentor' employee who knows how to do that job well, or . . . or . . . ." There are probably an infinite number of ways of working on the problem. Most of them might not be appropriate, but that still leaves plenty more to work with—provided a positive approach is used and negative talk is not permitted to shut down options and paint people into corners.

In countering employee negative talk, keep a sharp ear out for bipolar thinking. That's when someone talks about two options: either-or, or if-then, or yes-no, or go-no go. We humans have two hands, two eyes, two halves to our brains, and we easily think of two options. But with a little positive thinking it is also possible to come up with three options, or four, or ten. If the two obvious options are not highly appealing, then you want to encourage people to vocalize more options.

Many daily workplace conflicts arise from negative talk based on only two options. For instance, imagine that an employee comes to you complaining that another employee has scheduled his preferred vacation time the same week that she wanted to go. But now she can't go, since at least one of them needs to be in the office to cover their department's work. She says, "He always gets his first choice for vacation, and I don't care if he's already made travel plans. It's my turn to choose, and I want to take that week off instead of him."

This conflict arises over negative talk and negative thinking that sees the options as a simple either-or. As their manager, you might resolve it in favor of one or the other of them by doing whatever you think is fair. But the result of any either-or outcome will be that one loses and the other wins—so the overall satisfaction won't be high and you will have at least one disgruntled employee.

Instead, you might want to ask questions that encourage them to open up the discussion to other options. To see other options in this (or any) conflict, people need to look beneath the surface of their demands and explore their underlying reasons for making those demands. Underlying interests tend to be open ended—there are usually multiple ways to satisfy them. So you might start by steering the conversation toward the two employees' reasons for wanting the same week off.

Once you and they understand those reasons better, it may well be possible to come up with some additional options. For all you know, one wants to go to a music festival that starts on Thursday and the other wants to have Monday and Tuesday off to take a long weekend and go to a family wedding. If so, then they can easily split the week.

Or the answer may be more complicated, but still, there are likely to be many options once you get them talking positively about alternative approaches to their conflict. And when you do get your employees to explore positive options and avoid narrow trade-offs, you are stimulating positive talk and fighting against motivation-draining negative talk in every aspect of work, not just the specific conflict or problem at hand.

3. Victimized vs. In Charge

This kind of negative talk is about whether we feel victimized or whether we feel in charge of the events in our lives. Psychologists talk about these attitudes in terms of "locus of control," which is a fancy way of saying that, depending on your attitude, you may feel that control over your life is located within your reach or beyond it. When people talk about how bad things happen to them and they can't do anything about it, that negative talk tends to spread the attitude that we are not in charge and are unable to change situations. In the workplace such negative talk encourages employees to feel like things are happening *to* them and they are just hapless victims. And that is a debilitating attitude that saps motivation and hurts initiative and productivity.

A CASE IN POINT

Imagine you are talking to an employee about her work on a cross-functional team. The employee has just returned from a meeting, and when you ask her how it went, she says, "They keep loading me down with work because I'm the most junior person on the team. It's not fair but there's nothing I can do about it. You can't help either because the team leader is from headquarters."

Our most common responses to a comment like that are, one, to jump in and try to rescue the employee, or two, to distance ourselves from a whiner by just saying something sympathetic and turning our attention to something else. In other words, we tend to react to people who present themselves as victims by either helping them or avoiding them. In fact, this same reaction characterizes our response to someone who is begging for spare change on the street. *Rescue* or *abandon* is the basic choice that victimization talk engenders.

But from a motivational perspective, neither response is very helpful. The employee who is using this negative talk is not much use to herself or your organization in her current frame of mind, and her negative attitude may contaminate others as well. Ideally, you want employees to take a proactive approach to solving their problem. As long as she sighs and accepts her lot, her work and yours will suffer. So how can you rephrase her negative talk and get her into a frame of mind where she is willing and able to resolve this problem productively?

When countering victim-oriented negative talk, it is always good to ask questions that stimulate employees to think about how they might gain some control over the circumstances. For instance, you might say to the employee whose team leader has dumped extra work on her, "Is it possible for you to talk to the team leader alone about this problem?" or "Do you think the team knows that you are doing more work than anyone else—can you think of some way of measuring that and giving them information to guide their allocation of work in the future?" Questions such as these will encourage her to imagine ways of taking personal charge of trying to fix her problem.

You might also say something like, "Have you thought about ways in which I as your manager might be able to help you communicate with the team leader and resolve this issue? What are some options?" This question is not an offer to rescue her (which would perpetuate her feeling of being a victim). It encourages her to think of ways to use you as a resource in a self-rescue plan. That's a subtle but important difference, and as a manager you need to recognize the difference between being available as a resource for employees and rescuing them. Yes, you want to help them solve their problems. But when you do, make sure your approach involves *their* taking initiative, not just sitting on their hands while you charge in to the rescue!

The employee in the above example might respond to your questions by saying, "Well, you know, I don't feel comfortable complaining about it in the team meetings with everyone there, and most of them are from headquarters so I don't know them very well. But if I could have a one-to-one meeting with the team leader, maybe we could discuss the problem. But I don't want him to think I'm a whiner, so would you mind making the initial contact to make sure he realizes there is a real problem and ask him to discuss it with me? Then I think I'd feel comfortable meeting with him about it."

When you move an employee from talking as if she is a helpless victim to talking about productive steps to try to work on her problem, you are literally doing empowerment. Empowerment has been a buzz word for so long that we've almost forgotten what it means, but it simply means helping someone feel powerful enough to take initiative to solve problems and do their work better. When you transform negative attitudes, you are empowering employees to take charge of their working lives.

4. Blaming vs. Understanding

This kind of negative talk is about the "blame game" in organizations. Whenever you hear people judging or blaming themselves or others, you know you need to transform their negative statements into positive ones in a hurry. You can do so by encouraging them to seek a broader understanding of root causes.

There is a catchphrase from the total quality movement that expresses this strategy: "Blame the process, not the person." The idea is that while someone may have done something "wrong" or "bad" or made a mistake, if you want to truly learn from that experience you will ask why this could have happened, not who is to blame. When you seek the whys instead of the whos, you identify causes that you can modify to prevent problems in the future.

For instance, if a factory production line gets behind, the shift manager might say, "Who is responsible? I want the names of the employees whose workstations slowed us down." This is a blame game, and it is not likely to improve the production process and prevent slowdowns in the future.

In quality engineering, managers are taught to ask a different question: "Why did this happen? Which aspects of our production process make us vulnerable to this kind of slowdown, and what can we do to redesign them so it won't happen again?" This question encourages thoughtful, proactive suggestions from employees instead of putting them on the defensive. It is an example of positive talk, while the traditional "who did it?" approach is a classic example of negative talk. The benefits of transforming the blame game can be had in other areas beyond quality management too.

Do you want to know "who's responsible" when something goes wrong? Do you "beat yourself up" when you make a mistake? Or do you try to turn such situations into constructive learning experiences? That is the general issue to consider whenever talk turns to who done it. If you ask questions such as, "Why do you think this happened?" and "I wonder why they keep turning these in late? Is there anything we can do to streamline the work flow?" you will be transforming blame-oriented negative talk into positive talk about how to make it easier for people to get it right in the future.

A CASE IN POINT: WHY DID HE FORGET?

Imagine that you manage a forgetful employee named Chris. He is very bright and works hard, but often forgets to do things. Yesterday he said he was going to stay late to finish up several projects, so you reminded him to close up the office and turn off the lights when he left. When you came in this morning, the lights were on and the coffee pot had been left on all night. The coffee evaporated, and the pot cracked. And on top of that you realized that he had forgotten to submit an important report to you last week.

Your first reaction is to give Chris a piece of your mind, and maybe even to file a disciplinary report on the incident. You are good and sick of his forgetting things. He just isn't reliable enough to do his job well. But before you do anything, it occurs to you that as you think about the situation you are using negative talk. You are about to play the blame game, and if you do that with him, you will probably not make him any less forgetful—and you might encourage your employees to play the blame game too.

Instead, you decide to switch from thinking about "who done it" to thinking about *why* he did it and what could be done to keep him from forgetting important things in the future. Once you have some ideas yourself, you can talk to him more positively about his forgetfulness and ask *him* to think of his own list of controllable causes and actions to take.

Exercise 9-3. Controllable reasons for employee forgetting to do things.[3]

Take a minute to think of possible causes of his forgetfulness. Emphasize those causes that you and he *have control over*, and that you could fix in order to prevent him from being forgetful in the future. (Hint: It isn't productive to list "He's forgetful" as a cause since you aren't going to change that!)

Sample Solutions

▶ Chris apparently does not work from a written list or checklist—you could get him to use some sort of system.

▶ You give him verbal instructions—maybe written would be better.

▶ He is working independently—you could team him with a less forgetful employee.

▶ He may be thinking about and doing many things at once—you could ask him to complete one task before starting another.

▶ You aren't checking up on him to see whether he remembers to complete tasks—you could supervise him more closely.

▶ He is not using memory aids—you could insist that he create reminder notes for himself and that he post them where he can't miss seeing them.

▶ He may be overtired—it seems like he is working longer and harder than other employees.

5. Conflicting vs. Cooperating

Conflicts hurt motivation. They encourage people to blame each other and expend negative energy on their disagreements instead of focusing on how to move forward. And they often leave people with hurt feelings, which get in the way of a positive attitude toward their work. An employee who has been in a disagreement or conflict of some kind during the workday will come home thinking about the conflict and will often feel angry, hurt, and unhappy. Many employees call in sick the next day because they don't want to face the person or people they had the conflict with. Conflicts have strong but often hidden effects on work motivation and performance.

Conflicts and disagreements generate a lot of negative talk in workplaces. You can easily pick up the sounds of conflict by tuning your ear to negative talk. Whenever people label others' behaviors, for example, that is a sign of an unhealthy conflict. *Labeling* is when I tell you that you are being unreasonable, or that you don't care, or that you are always late, or that you never help out when I need it, or that you are inconsiderate. Whenever one person labels another, telling them what they are or are not doing, it irritates the other and breaks down communications. So labeling is an example of negative talk that you need to watch out for.

How do you counter labeling and other conflict-oriented negative talk? The general strategy is to encourage people to *shift from telling to asking*. If one person does not like what another person does, they need to ask why the person did it, not tell them what they did.

A CASE IN POINT

Imagine Rick complains to you that Zoe is lazy and takes too long coffee breaks. And Zoe complains to you that Rick is impossible to work with because he is rude and inconsiderate. What are you going to do to bring the two together and get them cooperating again?

First you need to dig through their negative talk and find out what is really going on—or better yet, get *them* to find out. Why does Rick care about the length of Zoe's coffee breaks? And why does Zoe think Rick is inconsiderate and rude? If you ask enough questions, you may learn something such as the following:

> ▶ Rick sits near Zoe's desk and feels he has to take her phone calls when she is away from the desk. But this interrupts his work and makes him irritated, so he resents it whenever she takes a break.
> ▶ Zoe recalls that Rick told her she was lazy and inconsiderate when she came back from an unusually long break a few days ago, and this labeling of her behavior made her upset so that now she won't speak to him.

Welcome to the effects of negative talk in conflict! These two have managed to shut down communications just when they need to communicate most. To open them back up and get them communicating you will have to harness the power of understanding. Whenever we can understand why the other person behaved as they did, we are able to get past our defensive or angry reactions and communicate more constructively about the conflict.

In this case, a series of questions in a meeting with both employees might soon reveal that Rick feels he has to handle the phone calls because the new automated answering system does not include all the right options needed to handle calls that come into the department. If that problem were fixed, he wouldn't have to cover for Zoe (and she wouldn't have to cover for him). They could just let the calls go to the answering system. Or there might be other options. Perhaps they could get portable phones and take them down to the coffee room when important calls are expected.

Similarly, your questions might soon reveal that Zoe is upset by being called lazy, and that Rick only said this because he was frustrated about the telephone problem. Zoe might find that she would have felt angry too in the same circumstances, and the whole thing will blow over quickly—provided you harness the power of positive talk and don't let them continue to discuss their conflict in a negative manner.

In your own interactions with employees, fellow managers, and your superiors in the workplace, you no doubt encounter numerous conflicts. You can apply the power of positive talk in these conflicts, and your example will spread the practice to your employees.

But if you fall into familiar negative-talk habits in conflicts, your example will reinforce these negative patterns in your people.

So it is important to ask yourself whether you are letting natural defensive and aggressive responses take control, or whether you are actively trying to sidestep conflicts by reaching out and seeking to understand and help with the other's party's needs. When you know you are in the habit of asking rather than telling, then you can be confident your employees will adopt this healthy habit as well.

They Aren't Attacking You (But It Sure Looks Like They Are!)

Managers have the hardest time avoiding negative talk when it is directed at *them*. It isn't fun to feel you are being attacked by your own people. Imagine any of these scenarios happening to you:

▶ You walk by an open office and overhear three of your employees complaining about you. One of them is saying that you have "really been a jerk lately." You don't know what the context of the comment is but the little bit you heard makes you angry and hurts your feelings.

▶ You learn that a new employee has been spreading negative information about you, telling the others that you don't work as hard as your employees do. She is encouraging the others to lobby for raises or bonuses to compensate them for their "extra" work. You know that the company is not going to increase salaries or give special bonuses right now, and you feel that she is going to spoil employee attitudes and sow the seeds of discontent. You are also angry that your own work ethic is being questioned, and you know that she has no idea how much work you bring home each night.

▶ You get a call from someone in the HR department who tells you an employee has come to them complaining that you "never listen" and won't give them the kind of assignments they want. You aren't sure who has been complaining about you, but you wish they had come to you first. It is upsetting when someone makes you look bad like that.

When things like this happen, managers feel like they are under attack. Their natural response is to react defensively. And the attack can easily leave them feeling depressed and less motivated about their work than usual. That's because managers are often the focus of negative talk. It comes with the position.

Understanding That You Are the Most Visible Target

Why are you likely to be the target of negative employee talk? As a manager, you are seen as controlling many aspects of your employees' working lives. It is natural for them to focus their frustrations on you. But of course it is not very productive or helpful. So don't be surprised when employees blame you or attack you—it's just a common form of negative talk, and it happens to every manager on occasion. But do apply your knowledge of negative talk and get to work transforming it to positive talk as soon as you can.

The first step in transforming negative employee talk about you is to recognize it as a symptom of underlying frustrations. Sure, their comments are attacking you, but that usually means there are some under-the-surface frustrations and you are the most visible target. If you take this negative talk at face value, you will get caught up in a cycle of negative talk and soon find yourself on the defensive—or even worse, attacking them. Even if you don't voice such negative responses out loud, you will probably voice them to yourself, and that is sufficient to give the negative talk power over you.

Using Your Skills to Transform Attacks

So how do you counter employees' negative talk about you in a positive manner? Apply all the same strategies you might use in transforming their negative talk about any other topic. The principles are the same, the topic is just a little more personal. But you can still transform the negative talk.

For example, suppose employees complain that you never listen. Rather than respond negatively with statements like "Well, you never tell me what's going on" or "My door is always open, you just never come to see me," you could transform the dialogue by asking them what they would recommend to improve communications. Encouraging them to come up with some options counters their negative talk in all five of the ways we've reviewed in this chapter. Specifically:

1. It encourages them not to accept the status quo, and it helps them see there are other ways to communicate with you.

2. It gets them out of the victim role and puts them in charge of solving the problem.

3. It ends the blame game and shifts their focus to understanding why the problem arose.

4. It expands their view of the options, expanding their initially narrow perspective.

5. It sidesteps their conflict-oriented approach and invites them to cooperate in solving the problem.

Summary

In this chapter you have learned powerful ways to transform negative talk and the negative attitudes that lurk beneath it. When you voice positive transformations of negative talk, you are able to work in simple and effective ways on the underlying attitudes that so often shape motivation and performance in the workplace.

Talk reflects and even shapes attitudes and thoughts, so working with negative talk is a way to manage for positive attitudes, initiative, and high workplace motivation. And when you come right down to it, talk *is* cheap, as the old saying goes. By working on negative talk and stimulating positive talk in your people, you can often do more to boost motivation than you could by using expensive incentives and rewards. It's the perfect business investment—virtually free and with a huge return in enhanced energy, empowered people, and improved performances. So what are you waiting for? Get out there and start talking!

Notes

1. For more details, see the *San Jose Mercury News*, January 18, 2002, p. 1E.

2. Based on Alexander Hiam and Helmi Pucino, *The Positive Talk Assessment and Negative Talk Transformation Activity*, copyright © 2000 by Alexander Hiam & Associates.

3. The exercise is based on the "Why T" activity in *The Wizard's Guide to Doing the Impossible* (Alexander Hiam & Associates, 2000).

CHAPTER 10

Appealing to Individual Motives

The magazine *Sales and Marketing Management* recently reported an alarming finding: *Most managers don't have any idea what motivates their employees*. Why not? Because they don't realize their employees might have unique motives. They just assume their employees must want the same incentives that they themselves want. This is an interesting insight and one that most managers do not fully appreciate. As a manager, it is easy to fall into the trap of giving your people the incentives that you would want—only to find many of your employees do not seem to be very motivated.

Each Individual's Work Motives Are Unique

So far in this book we have looked at factors that are universal. Everyone needs good communications, a positive emotional framework, and good feedback. And opportunities motivate everyone (but *which* opportunities are motivational to *which* employees?). In this chapter, we are going to look at the variation in employee work motives in order to give you the ability to adjust your approach for individual needs and preferences. In light of the finding mentioned above, this could be a very useful skill.

The problem with treating everyone the same is that everyone comes to work for unique reasons. So treating all employees the same is guaranteed to turn many of them off. The golden rule—do unto others as you'd have them do unto you—does not apply particularly well when it comes to management. Sure, you shouldn't treat your employees unfairly or inconsiderately, and your own sense of fairness and consideration can guide you as to what is right and wrong. But when it comes to knowing how to motivate your employees, you may need to treat them differently from how you yourself want to be treated.

For instance, how would you like to be rewarded for good performance by having to wear a fake royal crown all day? Well, personally I wouldn't like it one bit. I'd find it embarrassing and humiliating, and I'd resent the manager who pushed the silly scheme on me. I'd keep my head down and try not to be the winner. In the long run, I'd probably dust off my resume and look for another job.

But some employees respond very well to that particular incentive. It offers a high degree of public recognition, and it also appeals to one's competitive spirit. So a competitive employee who likes recognition may well be motivated by it. It's not likely to work for those of us who happen to be noncompetitive and motivated more by personal achievement than public recognition.

That *Sales & Marketing* report mentioned above goes on to tell the story of a Wendy's restaurant where the fastest register operator gets to wear a big gold crown—and as a result all the register operators are eager and quick to help and there are never long lines. So that incentive apparently works for that particular group of employees. But don't expect all employees to want to win the chance to wear a crown for the day. Some won't like that idea at all and will actively try to avoid doing too good a job so as to avoid the embarrassment. You have to get to know your people well enough to make sure you get a good match between incentives and individual preferences.

Exercise 10-1. Deciding how to reward Joan.

You have two options for recognizing the hard work and special contributions of Joan, the employee mentioned in earlier chapters who has been handling a heavy load of work. You know it is appropriate to offer Joan some kind of special thanks and recognition for all her hard work, but you aren't sure which of the following is most appropriate:

▶ *Option 1:* You could give her a gift certificate to a local department store. Your company recently bought some gift certificates for situations like this.

▶ *Option 2:* You could make up and present a special plaque honoring her and thanking her for her service to the company. You have a program on your computer for customizing and printing out certificates of appreciation, and you could easily mount one in a nice frame and give it to her at the next staff meeting.

In trying to decide between the two options, you have made some notes about Joan and what you know about her as an individual. You recall that she is friendly and generous with her coworkers, that she headed up the office's last two United Way fund-raising drives, and that she seems to take considerable pride in the company she works for and its high-quality products and services. She drives an older, faded-looking car and does not seem to be very much into image. You think she prefers to spend her money on travel and time with her friends. She sometimes hosts parties for the department and often brings in baked goods to share with her coworkers.

You know this is not a lot to go on, but perhaps there are some clues to help you select the most meaningful option as you decide how to recognize Joan's contributions. Which do you choose?

▶ *Option 1:* Gift certificate to department store
▶ *Option 2:* Certificate of appreciation presented at department meeting

Sample Solution

Option 2 is more likely to be meaningful to Joan. It will appeal to her because she seems to be motivated by affiliation with her associates and company. Rewards of financial value will probably not be as motivating to her as she does not seem to be very consumer-oriented.

Fitting Incentives to Individuals

The principle of individual incentives holds true for just about any-thing a manager or company might do to try to boost employee performance. For instance, take the ubiquitous suggestion system. The idea is that employees will submit great money-saving or reve-nue-generating ideas in exchange for the opportunity to win recog-nition or a prize. Now, who is going to be turned on by these rewards? People who like public recognition and competition, and people who are eager to enrich themselves with monetary re-wards—since that is what the system uses to motivate people to participate. Some people will respond well, since we know such people exist. After all, some of them are even willing to wear crowns behind the counter at a Wendy's restaurant.

But we also know that there are many other people who are motivated by opportunities to be creative or by opportunities to feel good about personal achievements, to name two other relevant work motives. And these two motives when combined are a potent source of fresh new ideas and suggestions. But you won't engage these people with a suggestion system that emphasizes recognition and reward and that is designed to be competitive. Most of them simply will not submit any ideas. The system doesn't appeal to their core work motives. And so it *excludes* many of the people who might provide the best ideas and suggestions.

How do you get around that? One solution is to give "winners" whose suggestions are chosen a wider choice of rewards. For exam-ple, someone who is achievement-oriented might like to have the chance to be in charge of implementing the idea.

Or think about the conventional ways of motivating sales forces. Salespeople are almost always given strong monetary incentives, combined with competitive prizes. These incentives appeal to peo-ple who are most strongly motivated by a desire to accumulate wealth combined with a desire to win the game. Competitive, re-ward-oriented people, in other words, traits that traditionally would have applied to the majority of salespeople. But today, the sales role is different in many organizations. It is more team-oriented, more technical, more consultative. And therefore different sorts of people fill the sales ranks in many organizations—people who have different incentive profiles and who may not respond to the traditional management approaches.

If their managers were to offer a broader selection of incentives, they would greatly improve the fit of their programs to their people. And they would find it far easier to boost performance and keep top salespeople from leaving. And if you as a manager find yourself working with salespeople, you will do well to identify which salespeople need other sorts of incentives, and then make a point of offering opportunities appropriate to their motives. (We will learn how to do that later in this chapter.)

Be Careful Not to Demotivate by Mistake!

What motivates one person may demotivate another. In my work on employee motivation, I have identified fifteen different work motives that are fairly common in the workplace—and found that most people are oriented strongly toward just one, two, or three of these. On average, a particular incentive or motivator may have a strong appeal to between a third and one-half of employees. And it will have little effect or even a negative effect on some of the rest of them. Managers who treat and motivate their people the same are accidentally turning off some of their employees.

Personality and Motivation

Personality is the unique temperament each individual brings to work. It is partially inborn and partially the result of experience, so it can and does change over time—but slowly over many years. It may also vary a bit by life-stage. For example, when people are just out of school and entering the workforce, they are in a stage of early adulthood that is oriented toward gaining experience, forming relationships, and building a career. Later, they may be raising children and worrying about a mortgage, and their priorities and interests will be different. But at any one period of time, the personality that each employee brings to work is a constant that you as a manager need to take into account.

To appreciate how important personality influences can be, consider for a moment your own personality. What are your most outstanding personality characteristics, and how do these influence your view of work? Are you risk-averse or a risk-taker? Do you like to compete or collaborate? Are you highly social or more of an independent worker? Personality variables such as these affect the way you react to many stimuli, and they can make some things into powerful motivators for you while making others ineffective.

As a manager, you need to make sure there is a good match to your employees' personalities as well as to their level of competence. You can improve the match between employees and opportunities—as well as the match between employees and rewards—by simply *thinking about* the individuals. You can also *ask* them what they want—sometimes the straightforward approach is best! And there is a third approach, which can help you and your employees refine your understanding of work motives and improve the quality of matches. It is to use a formal tool such as the *Incentive Profile*.

Using the Incentive Profile

To learn more about any individual employee's work incentives—including your own (which is a helpful thing in any career planning you may do)—you need to create an incentive profile. Like a lot of things in life, there is an easy and a hard way to do this, and the hard way produces more accurate results. If I were running a workshop or doing a consulting project for you, I'd take you through a detailed survey instrument to find out about your incentive profile. That is the most accurate way, but there is a shorter version too, and this "easy way" is reasonably accurate. Best of all, it only takes a minute.

In Exercise 10-2, you'll find a simple profile worksheet that you can use to compile your own incentive profile. You, like anyone, need to have the right sorts of projects and incentives and rewards that match your profile in order to feel good about your work. If you aren't getting them, then both you and your employer have a big problem. This chapter will show you how to solve that problem and many others like it.

Exercise 10-2. What is *your* unique incentive profile?

Read each statement and circle the appropriate number using the scale (from 1 = strongly disagree to 5 = strongly agree).

Motivators Some of these 15 incentives are important to you while others are not:	Rating 1 = strongly disagree 2 = disagree 3 = neutral 4 = agree 5 = strongly agree	Definitions To gain a better understanding of your higher-rated motivators, read their definitions below:
Affiliation	1 2 3 4 5	Desire to feel part of the group with which you work. Pleasure in being associated with a great organization.
Self-Expression	1 2 3 4 5	Urge to express yourself through your work. Creativity.
Achievement	1 2 3 4 5	Drive to accomplish personal goals. Pursuit of excellence.
Security	1 2 3 4 5	Need for stability or reduction of uncertainty and stress.
Career Growth	1 2 3 4 5	Urge to develop your career to its fullest.

Excitement	1	2	3	4	5	Impulse to seek new experiences and enjoy life through your work.
Status	1	2	3	4	5	Motivation to increase your standing through your accomplishments.
Purpose	1	2	3	4	5	Need for meaning and direction. Desire for important work that really matters.
Competition	1	2	3	4	5	Competitive spirit. Desire to excel in relation to others.
Recognition	1	2	3	4	5	Need for positive feedback and support from the group. Desire to be appropriately recognized for your contributions.
Consideration	1	2	3	4	5	Preference for a friendly, supportive work environment where people take care of each other.
Autonomy	1	2	3	4	5	Need for more control over your own working life. Desire for choice of working conditions or other options.
Rewards	1	2	3	4	5	Motivation to earn significant rewards or wealth from one's work.
Responsibility	1	2	3	4	5	Motivation to play a responsible leadership role in the workplace or society as a whole.

Personal needs	1 2 3 4 5	Need to satisfy essential personal or family priorities.

Now review your answers to identify the one or several highest scores. Which statements do you agree with most strongly? These correspond to your strongest work motives, which are named in the first column of the form.

Understanding the Fifteen Work Motives

As you saw when you completed Exercise 10-2, the Incentive Profile looks at fifteen possible work motives, each one distinct from the others. By looking at so many possible incentives, the tool gives us a lot of insight into how individuals may differ. Let's take another look at each of those possible work motives to make sure they are clear:

1. *Affiliation* is defined as the desire to feel part of the group with which you work or pleasure in being associated with a great organization. Employees for whom affiliation is important will take pride in opportunities to represent their organization in the public eye. They will value group recognition—for example, an award for the most valuable team will appeal to them. And they will take pride in a cap or mug with the company logo on it.

2. *Self-expression* is defined as the urge to express yourself through your work and is often associated with creativity. Employees for whom self-expression is important will prefer individual to group opportunities and will enjoy assignments that give them freedom to "do it their way." They like to be recognized for new ideas and are turned on by opportunities to customize their workplace or to define their own roles.

3. *Achievement* is defined as the drive to accomplish personal goals and the pursuit of personal excellence through one's work. These employees love a good challenge and like to be recognized for their personal achievements. For them, the journey is more important than the destination, so you don't want to let them stagnate. They need a steady diet of new hills to climb! By the way, achievement is the strongest single job motive on average in many organizations.

4. *Security* is defined as the need for stability and the desire to minimize uncertainty and stress. These employees are thrown off balance by unexpected changes, and are motivated by clear rules and supportive management. Awards based on length of service appeal to these employees.

5. *Career growth* is the urge to develop one's career to the fullest, and employees who value growth are motivated by stretch assignments, learning opportunities, exposure to mentors, training, and anything else that contributes to their career path. If you can help them gain credentials and visibility, they will appreciate it. Their desire to grow is valuable to you as a manager, because you can harness this urge by giving them tasks that they see as advancing their career path.

6. *Excitement* is the impulse to seek new experiences and enjoy life. A surprising number of employees leave their jobs or simply stop doing a good job because the jobs are not exciting and they get bored. So this is an important motivator to keep in mind. Variety of assignments, opportunities to travel or work with different people, and cross-training all appeal to these employees and help scratch their itch for excitement. You should also consider putting them into exciting work spaces where there is plenty of cross-traffic and noise.

7. *Status* is defined as the motivation to improve your standing through your accomplishments, and many people have

a natural drive to increase their status through their work. Public recognition at a reward ceremony is great for these employees, and they also enjoy titles (so why not make up project-oriented titles like Team Leader, Meeting Chair, or Committee Chair?). These same people also tend to value office size and location. Moving someone from a cubicle to a private office (or, God forbid, one with windows) is also a great motivator. They will lose motivation if you present a task as if it is unimportant, so make sure they know that their work is significant.

8. *Purpose* is the need for meaning or direction, and it manifests itself in some employees in the form of a strong desire for work that really matters, not only to them but to the organization or society as a whole. Make doubly sure that these employees have a clear idea of why their specific assignments are important, and try to find ways for them to contribute to their favorite social causes as well. When recognizing and rewarding them, consider a company donation that they can give in their name to their favorite charity.

9. *Competition* is the spirit that leads employees to want to excel in relation to others. They will appreciate your setting the goal of being the best company or department, and they also enjoy chances to outcompete their associates or peers. A prize rewarded to the person who does the best will always appeal to them. (But it may turn other employees off. If this is an issue for you, stick with team-oriented competitive goals where everyone in your group is working to be better or do better as a whole. Then let your competitive employees lead the charge.)

10. *Recognition* is the need for positive feedback from the group. Some employees have a relatively strong need for recognition, and it is not hard to fill this need by giving

them plenty of positive feedback, as well as periodic public thank-you's and formal recognition or rewards.

11. *Consideration* is kindness and thoughtfulness toward others, and many employees have a need for it in their workplace. The traditional impersonal approach to management does not meet their needs, and for them you need to make a point of being more friendly, thoughtful, and interested in how they are doing and what they think and feel about things going on at work.

12. *Autonomy* (or personal control) is the need for more options and choices, and it can be a powerful motivator for everyone. For employees who have an especially strong need for more control in their working lives, you need to emphasize giving them lots of choices and options in order to motivate them. For example, if you let them decide in what order to do their assignments, they will be more motivated than if you simply tell them when to do which assignment.

13. *Rewards* motivate people who wish to acquire things of value, such as merchandise, and who are oriented toward accumulating wealth through their work. Opportunities to win cash or merchandise, to advance to higher-paying positions, or to win cash awards for the best improvement ideas are good incentives for these employees.

14. *Responsibility* is important to employees who hope to play an increasingly responsible and significant role in their work. Assign these employees tasks in which they must play a leadership role and make sure others do their part too. Recognize them when they take initiative and display responsibility for solving problems. And think about how over time they can advance to formal positions of responsibility in their work.

15. *Personal needs*—such as the need for a flexible schedule in order to deal with the demands of day care, a sick parent or spouse, or a very difficult commute—sometimes rise to the surface and become dominant for employees. And when personal needs are the top priority, anything you can do as a manager to help out will be highly appreciated. Employees motivated by personal needs will be very loyal to a job if it helps them meet those personal needs. So rather than view an employee's problem as a problem for you and your organization, you could look at it as an opportunity to build a stronger relationship and strengthen the employee's commitment to the job.

This may seem like a long list. But the good news is that for any individual, the list of top work motives is going to be much shorter. Usually there are just a few that matter most. Sometimes the top five motivators are important. But never all fifteen. You can zero in on the top motivators and discuss ways of satisfying them through work opportunities, management style, and incentives. In the rest of the chapter, you'll see how to identify which work motives are most important for an individual employee, and you'll review a simple method for identifying and accommodating the work motives of your employees.

An Average Incentive Profile

Exhibit 10-1 is a graph of the average results (means) from a sample of 85 employees. It shows you a typical composite profile and highlights the top six motivators (which may often pop to the top of your employees' profiles as well—that's why many of the methods taught in this course help you appeal to these most common work motives). It is helpful to keep this composite picture in mind when designing general policies or programs. As long as they aim at the higher-ranking motivators they will apply to most employees fairly well, but remember that each of your employees will differ from it to varying degrees.

EXHIBIT 10-1. An average incentive profile. ───────────────

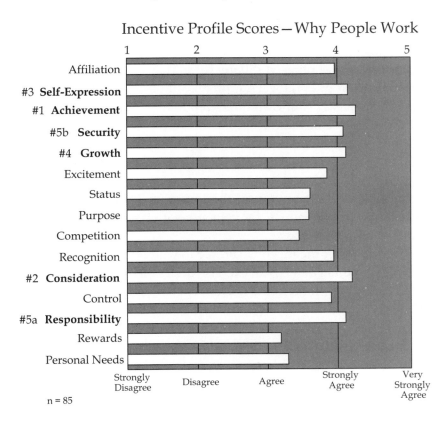

Incentive Profile Scores — Why People Work

Applying the Method to Your Employees

Each employee has a unique incentive profile, just like you do. One, two, or a few of the fifteen work motives are especially important to each individual employee. But which ones? When supervisors are aware of each individual's profile, they can better motivate and manage their people, and they can have more productive dialogues with them about what they need in order to perform at their peak.

As a manager, you can evaluate individual employees using the same scale you used to evaluate yourself. You can do this in two different ways. First, you can simply go through the fifteen motivators and rate the employees yourself, guessing how important each motivator might be to them. This approach relies on your judgment, and your judgment might be wrong. Exhibit 10-2 provides a blank form similar to the one you filled in for yourself in Exercise 10-2, except this one is phrased differently so that it can be used to describe one of your employees. (You may photocopy this job aid and use it in managing your own direct reports.)

By carefully considering each of fifteen different motivators, you are doing everything you can to make a thoughtful judgment. But if you still feel like you are unsure of your individual employees' incentive profiles, you can ask them for their direct input by administering the *employee version* of the Incentive Profile to them. It is reproduced in Appendix C for your use with your direct reports in your current job.

To administer the Incentive Profile to your employees, you need to explain to them that it is an exercise designed to help you provide better, more individualized management for them. You need to reassure them that:

1. You will not be keeping the form itself; *they can keep the findings* and only share them with you to the extent they are comfortable.

2. You will be inviting each of them to discuss their work motives in a *one-on-one meeting with you*, at which you will do your best to learn from the results of the survey and ask them for ideas about how to implement the findings to their benefit.

It is important to make these two points clear so that employees feel fully in control of their own incentive profiles. They will be happy about cooperating with you if they see this as an opportunity to explore their needs and interests with you, their manager. They will *not* be happy if they think you are forcing them to do a survey that may be used against them or is unlikely to benefit them personally.

EXHIBIT 10-2. Profiling your employees. ─────────────

You can use this form as a job aid to gain a better understanding of the key motivators for each of your direct reports.

Motivators *Some of these 15 incentives are important to them while others are not:*	Rating 1 = strongly disagree 2 = disagree 3 = agree 4 = strongly agree 5 = very strongly agree	Evaluation Statements *To gain a better understanding of employee's higher-rated motivators, decide how well each of these statements fits the employee in question:*
Affiliation	1 2 3 4 5	Wants to feel part of the group with which he/she works. Takes pleasure in being associated with a great organization.
Self-Expression	1 2 3 4 5	Has a strong urge to express him/herself through work. Creative.
Achievement	1 2 3 4 5	Driven to accomplish personal goals. Pursues excellence.
Security	1 2 3 4 5	Needs stability and reduction of uncertainty. Stressed.
Career Growth	1 2 3 4 5	Is eager to develop his/her career to its fullest.
Excitement	1 2 3 4 5	His/her impulse is to seek new experiences and enjoy life through work.
Status	1 2 3 4 5	Motivated to increase his/her standing through accomplishments.
Purpose	1 2 3 4 5	Needs meaning and direction. Wants to do important work that really matters.
Competition	1 2 3 4 5	Has a competitive spirit. Wants to excel in relation to others.
Recognition	1 2 3 4 5	Needs positive feedback and support from the group. Wants to be appropriately recognized for his/her contributions.
Consideration	1 2 3 4 5	Prefers a friendly, supportive work environment where people take care of each other.
Autonomy	1 2 3 4 5	Needs more control over his/her own working life. Prefers to have choices of working conditions and other options.
Rewards	1 2 3 4 5	Motivated to earn significant rewards or wealth from his/her work.
Responsibility	1 2 3 4 5	Motivated to play a responsible leadership role in the workplace and/or in society as a whole.
Personal Needs	1 2 3 4 5	Needs to satisfy essential personal or family priorities at the moment.

Negotiating Individual Incentives

What are your employee's needs, and how can you help provide them with work and a work environment that is optimal for their short-term performance and long-term development? These are the questions the Incentive Profile helps you answer. And it is easiest to answer these questions *with the employee*. So try to find a convenient time to take half an hour or more discussing the results of the Incentive Profile with each individual employee. Here are some questions that you can use in your discussion with the employee, to help you identify ways of taking action based on the results.

1. *Do your scores on the Incentive Profile reflect your priorities accurately?* It is important to make sure that employees agree with the results before you draw any conclusions based on them. If they see their motives differently, then simply go along with what they think. Work with whatever top motivators they say you should. It is their motivation, and the point of the profiling exercise is to help surface some useful ideas about what they are looking for in their work. So don't get into an argument—when it comes to what motivates them, assume that *the employees are usually right*.

2. *What are the most motivational aspects of your current job?* In pursuing this question, try to focus on ways in which the current work addresses the top-priority work motives. The idea is to start with what is good about the current situation and build from there, so it is important to be aware of any aspects of the job that align well with the employee's profile. These are to be preserved and if possible strengthened.

   For example, imagine that you have just sat down to meet with Juan, a young, eager, and helpful employee whose top incentive is responsibility. Juan agrees with this finding, saying that he does enjoy feeling responsible and is eager to take on additional responsibility over time.

   You ask him if any aspects of his work address this desire

for responsibility right now. He thinks for a minute, then says that his work as the point man for customer complaints is good because it makes him responsible for deciding how to handle problems and which resources or people to get involved. Now that you know this, you tell Juan you are pleased with the work he has been doing to resolve customer complaints and that you are willing to keep him on this assignment.

3. *What things are the most likely to hurt your motivation?* The point of this question is to make sure there are no "motivation-busters" in an employee's current situation. Anything that seems to run strongly counter to the top motivators might be demotivating and you will want to try to modify it if possible. For example, let's say that you ask this question of Juan—the employee from the above example whose profile is dominated by responsibility. And Juan points out that when he provides support for you, all his work is closely supervised and that you usually tell him how to handle any problems. This makes him feel that he has no responsibility.

You had not realized that this was an issue for him. Perhaps your style is a bit more directive than he likes. On the other hand, you explain to him that you are nervous about giving full responsibility to any relatively new employee, and it is important for you to make sure the work is done right. As a compromise, you suggest that Juan might try submitting proposed solutions to you, and that if you don't see anything wrong with them, you'll let him go ahead and do it his way. That way, at least some of the time he will be able to act on his own, and he will be getting more experience at taking responsibility for the work. If all goes well, he will be able to win the right to more and more responsibility of his own.

4. *Are there any things you'd like to change that would help you do a better job?* In answering this question, you and

your employee may find it helpful to refer back to the top motivator(s) from his incentive profile. The question provides an opportunity to explore what tasks are assigned and how they are assigned, what kinds of feedback systems are used, how much support he receives, how much flexibility he is given, what kinds of information you share with him, and what sorts of incentives or rewards you offer him for work well done and goals accomplished.

Try to keep the discussion focused on realistic ways of addressing top motivators. It is not productive to daydream about unrealistic things (you aren't going to double his salary just because he'd like more money, for example!). But on the other hand, with some creativity you may be able to find practical ways to address his fantasies—at least by taking small steps in the right direction.

A CASE IN POINT

Let's revisit Juan, the employee who wants to step up to increasing levels of responsibility over time. At first when you ask Juan what he'd like to change, he says he'd really like to be put in charge of a work group or team. You have to point out to him that he is younger and has less experience than many other employees, and that it is unfortunately unrealistic for him to expect such a promotion right away. But you also point out that it *is* realistic for him to set his sights on such a goal, and that you are pleased he wants to work toward it. Then you suggest that you and he spend a little time thinking about ways he could gain the experience and credentials needed to assume such a position of formal leadership.

After some discussion, the two of you agree that he would benefit from broader experience in the company, and he asks you to think of him next time a need arises for someone to help out on a project that might extend his knowledge. You also suggest that he might want to learn some management skills and discuss some options for him to get some training. Finally, you suggest that you might be able to assign him to assist the team leader on an important new project. The leader is an experienced manager who might be a good mentor for Juan, and while Juan would not have much responsibility of his own, he would have a chance to observe the manager in action.

(Although this example is set in a medium- to large-size organization, the same process can apply in principle in a smaller company. For instance, in a smaller business, Juan might be given a chance to work on the most important customer's account—with the owner of the business reviewing Juan's proposed actions before Juan implements them.)

5. *What things could I do differently to help you do a better job?* This is a great question because it gives employees a last chance to voice concerns that they may have found difficult to raise earlier. Many employees are wary when their manager calls them into a meeting to discuss their work. The "performance review syndrome" can set in, and employees may feel nervous or fearful that there is some hidden agenda. But by now, your questions should have made it clear that you simply want to do your best to make sure that their job is well fitted to them. So they may at this point bring up something a bit more personal or pointed.

And you may be offended by what they say!

For example, imagine that when you ask Juan whether there is anything you could do differently to help him do a better job, he replies, "Well, I guess it would be nice if you didn't always disagree with me in front of the others."

Wow. That's an emotionally loaded statement. It would be easy to get defensive and say something like, "What are you talking about? I never do that!" In which case, your opportunity to improve Juan's performance would end prematurely. So whatever the employee says, don't reply at first. Don't say anything at all. Try writing down their comment in order to give you time to process it, and to signify to them that you take it seriously.

Once you have waited out your initial emotional response, you may be in a better frame of mind to read between the lines and see what they *really* mean and need. For example, when Juan, who is motivated by a desire for increasing responsibility, says that his manager always disagrees with him in front of others, we can guess that he is sensitive to being overruled. He doesn't like it when his manager seems to be pulling rank on him. He may be oversensitive to this issue.

In fact, he most likely is oversensitive, since he used the word "always" in describing what his boss does. That's an emotional word, not a rational one. Nobody does something *always*. But it can seem that way if you are upset about the behavior. So if you were Juan's manager, you could deal productively with his (admittedly negative but still informative) reply by saying something like, "I don't mean to talk down to you, Juan, but I guess I am often in a hurry to take care of business so I express my opinion strongly. What would you like me to do?"

Juan might find it difficult to come up with a helpful suggestion—since in truth the situation he described is somewhat difficult to change. As his manager, you may sometimes override his comments. But on the other hand, there are certainly ways to minimize the problem he described. The most obvious step to take is to suggest to him that you and he discuss his work in private, when other employees are not listening. That way, you can tell him you disagree with a suggestion of his or give him other negative feedback without embarrassing him in front of his peers.

If you are not personally bothered by the kind of scenario Juan described, you may find it hard to appreciate his desire to avoid being corrected in public. You may even think that to go very far in business, Juan will need to develop a much thicker hide and not be so sensitive to criticism. But the whole point of the profiling process is to find out what motivates your employees *individually*—and how their motives may differ from your own.

So although you may not completely understand or even sympathize with Juan's feelings, you will still do well to try to take them into account when you manage him. That way you are adjusting your management to his top-priority work motives, instead of simply treating him like you would want a manager to treat you. He isn't you. His unique personality requires a unique approach to motivating him, and the incentive profile is a helpful tool as you explore his needs and adjust your style and his work assignments to his individual needs.

As the final step in the incentive profile process, you need to make some notes to record what you and the employee decided to do. A form such as the Incentive Profile in Exhibit 10-3 can be used for this purpose.

The Benefits of Appealing to Individual Motives

Sometimes it can seem like too much trouble to take the time to adapt your approach to the needs of individual employees. But there are good reasons to think that we could be doing a lot better at managing people than we usually do in business today. A little extra effort can and often does go a long way. Consider a few commonly accepted facts.

▶ Nearly 40 percent of all employees say their work is often or always stressful.

▶ More than half of all employees suffer from recurring sleeplessness.

▶ Most employees don't like their managers and feel that they are not well managed.

▶ Most companies report that turnover is too high and it is hard to retain their top performers.

EXHIBIT 10-3. Incentive Profile score sheet. ━━━━━━━━━━━━━

Incentive Profile*

Employee Name: [   ]

Date of Profile: [   ]

	Score →	3	4	5	6	7	8	9	10	11	12	13	14	15
1	Affiliation													
2	Self-Expression													
3	Achievement													
4	Security													
5	Career Growth													
6	Excitement													
7	Status													
8	Purpose													
9	Competition													
10	Recognition													
11	Consideration													
12	Autonomy													
13	Rewards													
14	Responsibility													
15	Personal Needs													

Create a bar chart by darkening or highlighting the rows up to the appropriate column for each score.

Notes & Ideas for Action:

_____
_____
_____
_____
_____
_____
_____

Tips: **Every answer is a right answer** on this assessment. Your goal as a manager is to gain insight (and help your employee gain insight) into what the employee's strongest motivators, needs, and goals are right now. These are the incentives that work needs to provide. How can you help make sure the employee's work *offers appropriate incentives*? How can you make sure work *does not conflict* with any high-priority incentives?

▶ A recent Gallup study concluded that about a fifth of all employees are so disengaged from their work that they do not even know what they should be doing or how to do it.

What gives? Why are employees still less happy and less productive than they could be, in spite of all the energy that goes into managing them? Certainly a part of the answer has to do with the way in which management traditionally ignores the unique differences between individual employees. Maybe it's because their managers never bothered to find out what makes each of them tick. And maybe it's time for managers to learn what motivates the people they work with, so that they can make sure everyone has the opportunity to get what they need in exchange for their hard work.

Summary

The methods of motivational management discussed in earlier chapters address universal motivators. Everyone needs good communications, a chance to participate and get engaged in the work, a good emotional climate in the workplace, clear goals and feedback, meaningful tasks that make a difference, and a level of challenge appropriate to their abilities so that they feel excellence is an achievable stretch.

Employees also like to reap rewards from their work. But what rewards? What are their specific career and personal goals when they come to work each day? Beyond the general principles of good management, there are many opportunities to get more specific and to treat each employee individually. Every employee has a unique set of work motives. Their priorities may be different from yours, and to manage them well you need to understand what they need. What are they seeking from their work?

The Incentive Profile can help you understand their needs and can be used to generate a productive dialogue with each employee about ways in which you can adjust their work and your approach as a manager to create a better match between their work motives and their work. That is an important step in maximizing individual performance, and it can do a great deal to minimize problems in the workplace and maximize performance and retention.

Note: It may be helpful for you to recognize that individual chapters in this book may be particularly relevant to certain motivators. For example:

▶ If you have employees whose profiles are dominated by *self-expression*, the participatory style of Chapters 3, Rethinking Management Communication, and 4, Using Motivational Communication Techniques, is particularly relevant to their needs, and they should respond well to the methods you learned in those chapters.

▶ The emotional intelligence–based methods of Chapter 5, Tackling the Feelings That Drive Performance, are particularly relevant to *consideration,* and employees who score high on that factor will respond well to that chapter.

▶ Chapter 6, Providing Challenging Opportunities, is especially relevant for employees who score high on *achievement, growth,* or *responsibility* dimensions of the Incentive Profile. And the Managing the Destination section of that chapter addresses the core concerns of employees who score high on the *purpose* dimension of the profile.

▶ Chapter 7, Using Feedback to Motivate, is especially relevant to employees *with high recognition, achievement, competition, purpose,* or *autonomy* scores.

▶ Chapter 8, Eliminating Contaminants, is important for those with high *consideration, self-expression,* or *affiliation* scores.

▶ Chapter 11, Using Recognition and Rewards, addresses the concerns of those with high *recognition, reward, affiliation,* or *achievement* scores.

Of course, all of these chapters address management methods that have universal appeal, but if you need to dip back into the chapters for ideas to help with specific employees, the key provided here will help you zero in and apply methods that have the most relevance based on their incentive profiles.

CHAPTER 11

Using Recognition and Rewards

Them here is a common misconception in management that recognition and rewards are the antidote to most employee attitude problems. If employees are not working hard enough, if they are making too many mistakes, if their attitudes are negative, if they are missing performance goals, if they are quitting in excessive numbers, then surely the problem can be fixed with a raise, bonuses, options, prizes, certificates of appreciation, a contest, or something of the sort. But usually it is not that simple.

Once when I was a guest on a business radio talk show, a guy who owned a car dealership called up and said, "I know how to motivate my employees. It's simple! I've decided to give all of them new BMWs to drive. That should guarantee that I have the most committed and motivated salespeople in the industry."

This was a nice windfall for the salespeople, but a terrible waste of money for the manager. It was not going to fix the problems he saw with employee motivation. His employees had some issues that needed to be addressed—for example, they did not feel they had enough control over how they did their work or enough information and responsibility. Giving them expensive cars to drive was not going to fix these underlying problems.

When to Recognize and Reward

As a manager, you probably won't have enough of a reward budget to blow money on new luxury cars for your employees, but you will most likely have *some* funding for rewards. Midsize and larger companies usually budget anywhere from $100 to $2,000 per employee for recognition and reward programs, and sometimes go far higher. Government offices and agencies tend to have smaller budgets—in the federal government it might be more like thirty dollars per employee. Nonprofits, local government offices, and small businesses may have no formal budget for employee recognition and rewards, but still on average they tend to spend at least twenty-five dollars per employee per year. And some small businesses go far higher—witness the car dealership story above.

Of course there is tremendous variation in the use of rewards and recognition programs from business to business, but it is interesting to look closely at one particular real-world case in which a large, far-flung operation, a district court system, found that cash awards were a positive factor for their people.

A CASE IN POINT

According to a careful study by Cameron S. Burke, Clerk, U.S. District and Bankruptcy Court for the District of Idaho: "Cash Awards programs have a positive affect on employee morale. This was reported by 74.8 percent of the respondents. Units noted that there was a drop in morale when cash awards were not funded. . . . Dividing the money is more common than believed and this has a very positive affect on employee morale. . . . Cash awards were most often given for the following reasons: sustained performance, work on special project and cost savings. . . . The mean award for those reporting was approximately $430."

In this organization (a U.S. district court with multiple locations in a state), the tradition is to give employees cash awards to recognize special service, and it would probably be bad for morale to stop the practice. (Once employees come to expect a cash award, it can be demotivating to take it away.)

Finding the Resources

Is there a "right" amount to budget per employee? Not really. Although realistically, if you don't have at least $100 per employee to play with, you are not going to have access to most of the commercial products and services that the incentive industry makes available for internal use with employees. For example, there are a host of business travel options, but of course you can't get an employee a plane ticket and a long weekend at a resort hotel for much under $750. But you can probably buy mugs with the company logo for five dollars per employee, so there is always something to choose from at every price level.

It is therefore surprising that not all employers use rewards. Yet employee rewards and gifts are not as common as you might think, according to the survey data in Exhibit 11-1. A little more than half of the companies surveyed give gifts. And, even more startling, only 12 percent of companies give employees birthday presents. That's a basic, traditional way of telling someone you value them, and it's not hard to come up with *something* you can give on every birthday. Again, your options are only limited by your imagination!

You can even do a great deal with a budget of zero dollars and

EXHIBIT 11-1. A statistical snapshot of employee rewards. ──────────

Here are a few facts about gift giving from companies to employees, according to a survey by Incentive magazine:

- ▶ 67 percent of companies give employees gifts.
- ▶ 58 percent of companies give gifts at the Christmas/Hanukkah season.
- ▶ 52 percent of companies give gifts for recognition and motivation.
- ▶ Only 13 percent of companies give gifts for other holidays, and only 12 percent for birthdays.

a little ingenuity. It costs you nothing to say thank you. It costs nothing to make up a nice Certificate of Appreciation on a computer and print it out and present it to employees at a gathering of their peers. It costs nothing to dust off some oversized old trophy from someone's attic, put a label on it, and make it into a humorous award for the team that did the most with the least. It costs nothing to circulate a thank-you note and collect signatures from everyone in your group to recognize an employee who made a notable contribution to a project or volunteered to do something helpful for others. So don't be hung up on the cost issue.

It also costs almost nothing to reward someone with time off—especially if you cover for them or if their peers agree to take up the slack. So if you can get access to budgeted funds, by all means use them (wisely—we'll see how, soon). But if there is no budget, don't worry. You still have imagination, and that's a true treasure trove when it comes to recognition and rewards.

You can also make a strong argument that money spent wisely on employee recognition and rewards, or even just on celebrations and parties for employees, will be more than offset by improved productivity and quality, happier customers, and better word of mouth. Herb Kelleher, CEO of Southwest Airlines, argues that his company's success is largely due to the way it treats its employees. He spends more than his competitors do on employee recognition and says, "Southwest Airlines has the best customer-complaint record in the American airline industry, and who can say how much that's worth? I could sit in my office one afternoon and cut Southwest Airlines' budget substantially by cutting these things. But that's like cutting out your heart" (*Inc.*, May 1998, p. 123).

Celebrating Employee Contributions

Herb Kelleher described an interesting approach to recognizing employee effort in an interview with an editor from *Inc.* magazine: "In the hallways of our headquarters, we have photos of our employees—about 1,500 pictures of our people engaged in various activities, being honored, given awards.

> Those pictures show that we're interested not in potted palms or in Chinese art, but in our people. It's another kind of celebration, and it's something that costs very little." (*Inc.,* May 1998, p. 123.)

Using Recognition and Rewards to Finish the Job . . . Not Start It

Earlier chapters explored a variety of techniques and tactics for building strong employee motivation. These are an essential foundation for any reward or recognition efforts. You can't create great performances by recognizing and rewarding them. You have to have great performances to start with so you have something worthy of recognition and rewards! That was the mistake the owner of the car dealership made—he assumed he could jump-start his employees' motivation with a single major reward. He didn't take the time to build strong attitudes and strong performances from the ground up.

But *you* understand the importance of good motivational management on an ongoing basis, so you won't make this mistake. You will work on employee motivation regularly in the way you communicate with employees and in the way you design and manage their work. So you will have positive attitudes and hard work in your group of employees. And when employees are motivated and try hard, it is a good idea to recognize and reward them for their initiative.

Recognize and Reward Effort and Initiative

In fact, the best use of recognition and rewards is for effort. When employees work hard, when they try hard to solve problems or achieve goals, make a point of letting them know you appreciate their effort.

Why effort? Don't most recognition and reward programs focus on results?

Well, yes, most programs do reward results rather than effort. But think about what you are trying to do. As a manager, you want

to, one, maximize healthy attitudes so your people are highly motivated to work hard and try their best, and two, translate the efforts
of your motivated employees into great results by giving them the
right work to do. So employees own the first half of the equation
and managers own the second half. And often, rewards tied to organizational performance do not feel very relevant or motivating to
employees, because they simply do not see tight links between their
effort and the rewarded results. The rewards don't seem to be very
controllable to them.

It is up to the managers of any organization to make sure the
strategy is good and the ship is heading in the right direction. So
if the results are disappointing, managers may deserve to feel the
pain—but usually it is employees who feel it instead. I much prefer
to focus recognition and rewards on the thing the employees can
control completely (with the help of good motivational management): their own performances. When you recognize and reward
effort, you are using recognition and rewards to reinforce all your
efforts to build high levels of employee motivation. You are focusing
specifically on what you need most from your employees.

There is another good reason to reward effort over results. It is
simply that on average, the impact is greater when you do. This is
nowhere more clear than in education, where a variety of studies
have shown that when a teacher (or parent) praises students for
their effort, they try harder and do better in the future. Recognizing
effort works well because it provides direct feedback about one's
attitude toward work. And remember that motivation is an attitude—an attitude that determines how hard and how well your employees work. So keep this in mind when designing recognition and
rewards and try to use them to highlight good effort and healthy
motivation whenever possible.

Here's a third reason. And you do need three good reasons to
emphasize rewarding effort, not results, because you will get some
flak from other managers who still believe in the traditional approach. The third reason to recognize and reward effort is that if

you put too much emphasis on recognizing and rewarding results, you are going down that extrinsic motivation path we went to so much trouble in earlier chapters to get off of. In short, you are holding out a carrot (and by implication a stick) to control people into doing what you want. It works much better to keep their intrinsic motivation in the fore and simply use recognition and rewards as a way to keep spirits up and maintain a positive, considerate management style by encouraging employees who are striving hard toward challenging goals.

In other words, use recognition and rewards (or just plain old gifts) to encourage people and to show them you appreciate their hard work—the hard work inspired by meaningful tasks that they are intrinsically motivated to pursue.

Frosting the Cake

With these basic parameters in mind, you can use recognition and rewards to layer some exciting or inspiring or just plain funny recognition and reward programs on top of that solid motivation foundation you built. I often refer to recognition and reward programs as the frosting on the cake. If you've baked a good cake, a good frosting will make it special.

But too often, managers forget about the cake and just slather thick frosting over an old, dry biscuit. When they still don't get a big response, they add decorative icing, fancy frosting flowers, and the like. But nothing they do seems to stimulate employees' appetites, because down under all that frosting something is old and dry or even rotten. That's why the average employee reward program is a dud, no matter how exciting the rewards. And that's why I've left this chapter on rewards until the *end* of the book.

Careful Not to Demotivate!

As a manager, you need to realize that many employees are suspicious or resentful of the formal incentives and rewards their companies and managers offer. The employees' most common complaint is that they feel like they are being treated like children. They sense the hidden threat that "you won't get the good things you want unless you knuckle under to our control." When this happens, the incentive program generates more negative than positive feelings. And when you have negative attitudes, this leads to resistance against any goals or changes, and you are on the path to extrinsic, not intrinsic, motivation.

A CASE IN POINT

A company was having lots of problems stemming from poor treatment of employees, and it was losing many of its best people because of pay and benefits cuts, loss of personal autonomy through centralization, and other serious issues. This company convened a meeting of employees to get at the roots of the problem. Employees bared their souls to management in the expectation of a serious fix. Then management announced the "solution"—they created The Fun Team, which would be in charge of arranging for an entertainment or fun event each quarter.

Talk about disillusionment! People were really infuriated. But on the other hand, I've seen that same concept of an employee team with a budget and mandate to put on fun events work well and receive a great reception—when underlying issues were taken care of first. Almost any program can be successful *or* unsuccessful, depending upon the context and how it's implemented. It's a delicate thing, and most managers don't realize just how careful they have to be when they design an incentive system or introduce a new reward.

When managers throw a reward program at demotivated employees, the employees react with cynicism, resistance, and withdrawal. They sense the disconnect between the talk and the walk. It angers them, and sometimes it even drives them off. Reward systems that look like two-dimensional movie sets don't work, and employees don't like them. Here are some comments from employees who didn't like their employers' reward programs:

▶ "They treat us like kids."

▶ "It's stupid, but we all go along with it. What else can we do?"

▶ "Once a month, they feed us well and give us prizes and awards. The rest of the time, they treat us like dogs."

▶ "Do they really think I'm going to work extra hours every day all year for a one in a thousand chance of going to Hawaii for the weekend?"

▶ "For every idea that gets a reward, thousands of suggestions are ignored. Is that supposed to motivate me?"

▶ "Right. Like I'm going to work harder for play-money coupons when I haven't had a proper raise in three years."

▶ "My boss used to leave me alone except when he wanted to chew me out. But ever since that training he keeps coming around and bugging me to 'catch me doing something right.' I don't want an insincere pat on the back from him. He doesn't know the difference between good and bad work anyway."

In each of these cases, managers have skipped over the essentials of building motivation, and have tried to frost an old cake with fancy new programs. The responses are predictable.

The trick is to align incentives with intrinsic motivation, and to make sure that those incentives represent success along a path that is accessible and obvious to all. Rewards are simply symbols. To find out whether they will work, ask yourself what they symbolize. If it's good stuff, then *any* symbol will do (although some will certainly do better than others). Just make sure any external incentives symbolize internal drive to achieve—not external control—by linking them to initiative and effort.

Showing Them You Care

Imagine that you have the choice of working for one of the following two managers. This is what you know about the two managers from your discussions with people who have worked with them:

▶ *Manager A*. She is known as tough and ambitious. She expects hard work and long hours from employees. But she does not take much personal interest in them, and they sometimes wonder whether she even remembers their names.

▶ *Manager B*. She is known as a considerate manager who expects a lot of her employees, but gives a lot of herself as well. She puts on lunchtime birthday parties for her employees, and she often takes the time to write a thank-you card or stop by and offer a word of thanks and a handshake to show that she appreciates your hard work.

Which of these bosses would you prefer to work with? Which one might be more likely to inspire you to do the best you possibly can?

Manager B's style is far more likely to earn her the loyalty and commitment of her people than Manager A's. Manager B knows that recognition and rewards are a simple, easy way to demonstrate that you appreciate your people and their efforts. Ongoing recognition and occasional "from the heart" rewards are essential to providing considerate management and showing you care. As Mary Kay Ash, founder of Mary Kay Cosmetics, puts it, "Make people who work for you feel important. If you honor and serve them, they'll honor and serve you."

As a manager, you can look at recognition and rewards as part of your basic "management manners" and use them as Manager B does, to show consideration and respect for your people and let them know you value their efforts.

Focusing on Specific Work Motives

In addition, you may want to use recognition or rewards to strengthen the appeal of a job to your employees by increasing the amount of a specific incentive they care about. Remember the Incentive Profile and its fifteen different work motives from Chapter 10? If you know that a specific employee or group of employees is motivated by, say, excitement, then it is a simple thing to add more excitement to their work by using appropriate recognition and rewards. For example . . . but wait, isn't this a great opportunity for an exercise?

Exercise 11-1. Adding excitement.

Imagine you have a group of employees who value excitement, and who sometimes feel their work is getting dull and repetitive. How might you use recognition or rewards to pump things up and add some fun and excitement to their workplace? Come up with at least three ideas:

1.

2.

3.

Sample Solutions

Here are some ideas, just for comparison. You could purchase one of those relatively inexpensive coupon books (with restaurants, stores, movie theaters, etc. included for a city), then cut out a dozen of the best coupons and put them in a box or hat or something and do a drawing in which each employee gets a coupon. Then you could have a bonus round drawing in which one of the employees wins an extra fifty dollars, which they could use in combination with their coupon. This is a kind of crazy approach, but it is fun, and I think it will be an amusing highlight to the week in which you do it.

You could also ask two of your employees to make up a scavenger hunt, hiding clues and prizes for the others. Or how about starting a bulletin board where people post candidates for the most exciting weekend trip or craziest vacation—and then have a joke prize you give out to the employee whose entry is voted best? All of these ideas emphasize fun, adventure, and excitement and will help excitement-oriented employees keep up their enthusiasm.

Each employee's incentive profile is dominated by just one or a few work motives, as you learned in Chapter 10. You can consult the table in Exhibit 11-2 to identify the types of recognition and rewards that have the highest impact for any employee based on their dominant work motives. (Use the Incentive Profile survey to find out what your employees' dominant work motives are. It's re-produced for your use in Appendix C.)

For example, someone who is affiliation-oriented will enjoy the gift or reward of an article of clothing with the company logo on it. If they are on a team or are part of a project, they will also enjoy products identified with a unique logo and name associated with their team or project. And they will enjoy opportunities to get to-gether socially with their work group. These ideas emphasize their association with the group. Consult Exhibit 11-2 for these and other ideas that are specific to each of the work motives.

You can apply the Incentive Profile to individuals by selecting recognition and reward ideas that match their dominant work mo-tives—and avoiding those that don't.

You can also apply the Incentive Profile to groups of employees by surveying the group and averaging their scores to create a com-posite profile. Then target the top three to five work incentives for the group as a whole in order to maximize the odds of motivating each employee in the group.

EXHIBIT 11-2. Work motives and matching rewards. ───────

Work Motive	High-Impact Recognition and Rewards
Affiliation	Logo-identified or group-identified merchandise of all sorts, including clothing and personal-use items like mugs. Recognition in group settings/ceremonies. Public/visible roles and recognition. Travel, parties, or retreats with the group.
Self-Expression	Coupons or gift certificates that permit freedom of choice. Recognition/celebration of unique individual accomplishments. Roasting-style recognition of unique personality and contributions. Posting or sharing of individual work.
Achievement	Recognition of exceptional individual achievements. Recognition of contributions to exceptional group achievements. Symbolic rewards (trophies etc.) to memorialize achievements. Appreciation, recognition from admired role models or mentors.
Security	Frequent small gifts or rewards to reassure employee that their work is still valued. Contributions to savings or retirement funds. Meals, massages, and sympathy.
Career Growth	Recognition of progress toward learning and career goals (such as certificates and plaques). Opportunities to attend career workshops or courses. Chances to work with a mentor or rotate into new areas for learning and personal development. Participation in events that facilitate professional networking. Subscriptions to professional publications.

(continues)

EXHIBIT 11-2. (Continued).

Excitement	Anything fun, such as travel, a night on the town, a change of location, or a temporary posting to a new area. Humorous awards and events. Celebrations. Tickets to entertainment events.
Status	Symbolic rewards such as trophies, use of the best parking space. Upscale/status-oriented rewards and gifts (watches, consumer electronics). Use of a luxury automobile. Trips to upscale resorts. Recognition of advancement in the company. Formal clothing. Participation in sporting events with a social dimension (such as a golf or tennis outing to a nice club).
Purpose	Recognition for contributing to an important project. Chance to participate in volunteer work for a worthwhile charity in the community. Matching gift program to leverage employee donations. Awards for progress toward major organizational goals (such as a quality improvement or customer service initiative).
Competition	Reward programs involving peer or team competition. Tough performance goals with prizes for those who achieve them. Lottery-style reward programs where your prize gives you a chance to win smaller or larger rewards. Recognition for best-of performance.
Recognition	Frequent thank-you's and small recognition and reward events. Thank-you and appreciation cards. Group award events.
Consideration	Thoughtful gifts and kind gestures. Rewards of time off. Concierge services. Thank-you notes, especially when signed by everyone. Any rewards or gifts that increase personal comfort. Warm clothing. Recuperation-oriented travel or services (spas, massages).

Autonomy	Time off or flexible schedules. Rewards of certificates or points that can be redeemed when and how employee chooses. Gifts of useful items for work environment that employee can place and control the use of (such as swing-arm lamp with dimmer or CD player with headphones). Travel options in which employee chooses when and where to go and who to go with.
Rewards	Bonuses, stock options, and other things of monetary value. Cash rewards. Merchandise with significant and lasting value. Chances to win money (lottery tickets, drawings). Commissions.
Responsibility	Recognition of advancement to positions of greater responsibility. Rewards tied to performance especially when employee takes on extra responsibilities. Public/peer recognition of responsibilities.
Personal Needs	Concierge services. Flextime. Coupons or gift certificates that can be redeemed for a wide variety of goods and services. Cash. Rewards of extra vacation or free days. Contributions toward insurance plans or health expenses.

Reproduced by permission of Alexander Hiam & Associates.

Exercise 11-2. Test your motivation skills.

A polo shirt with the name of the company embroidered on it would be an especially good gift for employees who are:

a. Affiliation-oriented
b. Self-expression-oriented
c. Excitement-oriented
d. Growth-oriented

Yes, that's right, "a" is the best answer. Any merchandise you might wear that identifies you with your employer or a special project team or location is clearly oriented toward affiliation. For those who take pride in the group they are working with, this is a great incentive. For others, it may not be very effective. (If you aren't sure who does and doesn't like affiliation-oriented rewards, try giving out a simple, inexpensive item of clothing or a coffee mug with a company logo on it—and wait to see how many employees actually use it visibly. Some will, but others won't.)

If you lack data on your employees, try targeting your incentives and rewards to these common work motives: achievement, consideration, self-expression, growth, responsibility, and security. As you learned in Chapter 10, they are generally the most common and powerful in workplaces, and rank in the top five in the composite incentive profile presented in that chapter.

Successful Rewards: The High Involvement Approach

How do you know if the recognition and rewards you provide are working?

Rewards work well when they stimulate high involvement on the part of employees. Specifically, employees need to be engaged with the reward or recognition system on two dimensions: rational and emotional. Only when you have high involvement on both dimensions do you get a motivational bang for your reward buck. In other words, a good reward or recognition event makes sense intellectually to the employee—they get what it is about and see how it relates to important workplace goals. And the recognition or reward event also feels good to them—it generates positive enthusiasm on an emotional level.

Banking on Recognition

Investor's Bank and Trust (Boston) uses two basic approaches to rewarding exceptional performers—approaches that many other organizations use and that are often quite effective. Their *Star Award* is a cash recognition award program for employees who perform above and beyond expectations. It is awarded based on manager ratings, so you can think of this as a centrally controlled way to reward employees. Their *Spotlight Award* is peer-based and so not directly controlled by managers. This program allows employees to recognize other employees for their accomplishments and hard work. It is a good idea to combine both these strategies, as Investor's Bank does. Sometimes managers aren't aware of the extra efforts of an employee, in which case a peer-nominated award or reward can fill the gap.

Reward and recognition methods that do *not* win employee involvement on either the rational or emotional dimension will not get any attention. They will tend to be ignored. But it could be and often is worse! If you generate involvement on only one of the two dimensions, you will get some attention but it won't add up to a positive response. You are likely, in fact, to see inappropriate or even negative responses to the rewards. They won't have the desired effect, and they may have other less desired effects.

If a reward gets lots of emotional involvement but little rational involvement, you will get employees' attention. But the effect will not be specific to the behaviors you wished to stimulate and reward. And that's potentially dangerous, because you will have aroused their emotions in a nonspecific and uncontrolled manner.

A CASE IN POINT

Take the example of a company that decided to do something about slipping sales quotas by offering a very expensive and attractive two-week trip to the Caribbean for two to the salesperson who sold the most in the next six months. This prize was highly coveted. Everyone wanted it. Everyone's spouses or significant others wanted them to win it too. So there was plenty of emotional involvement.

But despite this high emotional involvement, the contest hurt motivation and generated negative attitudes in the sales force. Why? Because

> the rational side wasn't well thought out. Salespeople faced many new competitors, and the company didn't give them tools or strategies to improve their sales, so they felt unclear about how to win the prize. In addition, there were fairness issues, because some territories had more sales potential than others, and the contest didn't take this into account.
>
> Finally, some of the salespeople worked in teams, and were not sure how their individual efforts might or might not be counted in the contest. These problems made the salespeople question the contest on rational grounds, and spoiled the motivational impact of it. Even the person who won the trip didn't feel that good about it because she worried that the contest had been arbitrary and unfair.

When you take care of the rational side and work out rules and methods that are fair and accurate and obey all the rules of good feedback, then you can build the kind of rational involvement needed to make a reward motivational. But again, you have to take care of the other dimension too. A rational, well-designed sales contest with an emotionally boring and unappealing prize won't work either. People will say they know they ought to get up for it and try their best, but they just don't seem to feel like it. They will lack the inspiration that emotional involvement provides.

Testing Your Reward or Recognition Plans

How do you know whether a reward or other recognition method will work? Easy. Just find out whether employees view it as both rationally and emotionally involving. If they do, then you know your reward takes the high involvement approach to motivation and will be effective. The test says it will work because it *makes sense* and it also *feels good*.

Exhibit 11-3 is a simple instrument for testing the appeal of a reward or recognition event or program. It is useful when you are evaluating or designing a specific recognition or reward program, so you might want to save it for later use. This version is designed to be filled out by you, the manager or supervisor, but similar ques-

EXHIBIT 11-3. Job aid: Testing the appeal of a reward. ───────────

Choose yes or no

yes   no   1. Do employees know exactly what behaviors the reward
                    is supposed to encourage?

yes   no   2. Do employees believe that they can control the results
                    upon which the reward is based?

yes   no   3. Is the reward given quickly enough for employees to
                    remember what it is all about?

yes   no   4. Does the reward encourage behaviors that are also
                    encouraged by managers on a daily basis?

yes   no   5. Does the reward encourage behaviors that are also
                    encouraged by the organization's rules and systems?

yes   no   6. Does the reward encourage behaviors that are also
                    encouraged by employee compensation systems?

yes   no   7. Does the reward encourage behaviors that are also
                    encouraged by formal performance review systems?

yes   no   8. Is the reward consistent with other reward and
                    recognition programs?

yes   no   9. Is the reward consistent with the ways in which
                    employees are trained?

yes   no   10. Is the reward consistent with the ways in which
                     employees are managed?

yes   no   11. Is the reward consistent with the organization's top-
                     priority development goals?

yes   no   12. Is the reward consistent with employees' personal
                     development paths and goals?

Now stop and tally your scores for the first dozen questions. How many "yes"
answers did you circle? _____ = **Rational Involvement Score.** Please
make a note of it.

Now complete the instrument by answering the next set of questions:

yes   no   13. Is the reward fun in employees' eyes?

yes   no   14. Is the reward exciting to employees?

(continues)

EXHIBIT 11-3. (Continued). ─────────────────────────────

yes	no	15. Is the reward highly desirable to employees?
yes	no	16. Do employees feel positive about their work in general?
yes	no	17. Do employees feel in control of their performance results?
yes	no	18. Do employees receive more positive than negative feedback in general?
yes	no	19. Do employees feel very little or no fear about their work situations?
yes	no	20. Do employees feel that the reward symbolizes good personal opportunities for growth and development at work?
yes	no	21. Do employees feel that there is open, honest communication between managers and employees?
yes	no	22. Do employees feel confident of their ability to do the rewarded things well?
yes	no	23. Do employees feel optimistic about their work?
yes	no	24. Do you feel good about the employees this program rewards?

Finally, please tally your scores for the second dozen questions (numbers 13 through 24). How many "yes" answers did you circle? _____ = **Emotional Involvement Score.** Please make a note of it too.

───

tions can also be asked of employees to check that they see the reward the same way you do.

Interpreting Your Score to Increase the Reward's Impact

Will a particular reward work? Will it be received with enthusiasm and will it boost employee motivation—or will it generate cynicism or lack of interest and fail to increase motivation and performance levels significantly? It depends on your scores on the two sets of questions in Exhibit 11-3.

Here are the score ranges. Use them to help interpret your scores by converting them from numbers to levels:

| *Number of*
Yes Answers
(out of 12)	*Level:*
1–4	Low
5–8	Medium
9–12	High

Using this scale, interpret your results from each of the two sets of questions.

Set 1 (Questions 1 to 12): My Rational Involvement Score is _____.

Set 2 (Questions 13—24): My Emotional Involvement Score is _____.

Make a note as to whether your scores are low, medium, or high on each of these two measures.

If a current or planned reward or other recognition program scored *high* on both rational and emotional involvement, you've got a winner! But most do not, at least at first. If you scored medium or low on rational involvement, review the feedback mechanisms to make sure the reward and other feedback is clear, accurate, and timely. Check to see that there are clear paths between employee behavior and results. Also check for consistency with organizational goals, other rewards, and employee requirements and instructions. Use the questions in the instrument to help you target specific problem areas.

If you scored medium or low on emotional involvement, then employees are not likely to become emotionally engaged with the reward in question. You need to check the many contributors to emotional involvement, including the baseline emotional state of employees, the emotional appeal of the reward itself, and other factors that the second set of questions will help you identify. Basically, any "no" answer on either set of questions signals a very specific problem area that may sabotage your reward.

Effective Recognition and Reward at Unisys

The Unisys Shared Service Center in Bismarck, North Dakota, handles a lot of back-office functions, from paying bills to photocopying resumes from job-seekers. These might sound like thankless tasks, but the employees are known for their dedication to customer satisfaction and cost savings and have set a high standard for other units throughout Unisys. How come?

Well-designed recognition and rewards are one reason for the success of this group of employees. Bonuses are available for everyone when the unit performs well, and more than that, there is a culture of recognition and celebration to reinforce the monetary rewards with a sense of pride in accomplishment. At one of their year-end ceremonies, the employees were praised for their efforts not only by their general manager but also by guest speakers, including the state's lieutenant governor and a visiting expert on customer service.

And throughout the year, managers emphasize not just doing the work but improving the quality of the work. Employees work in teams and have specific improvement goals to challenge them. There is an excitement to the work because of management's vision for the facility: Unisys General Manager Tom Severin was quoted as saying that "Our vision calls for us to be the superior provider of back-office accounting functions" (quoted in the *Bismarck Tribune*, February 20, 1997). And their efforts to achieve that goal receive multiple forms of recognition, which helps keep enthusiasm up. The center has won several awards for excellence, including two national Reach awards.

Summary

The Introduction and first chapter of this book opened with a look at the broader sweep of change in the field of management and the resulting need to manage for employee performances that feature a high degree of initiative, enthusiasm, effort, creativity, and collaboration. These are the attributes we need to see in order to succeed in what I term a level-two economic environment, in which change and challenge is commonplace.

In a more traditional level-one environment, I might have started this book with a chapter on recognition and rewards. As long as the fundamentals of management are sound and do not need to be reexamined, there is no reason not to leap directly to recognition and reward when thinking about employee motivation. The problem comes when the fundamentals of management are not aligned with the current performance requirements. Then the obvious approaches to motivation through incentives and recognition are not going to work.

First we have to rethink the way we communicate with employees, the way we structure work, the way we and they feel about the work, and other important elements of the basic performance environment. When these elements are aligned with our performance requirements and goals, then we can reinforce them with good incentives. Recognition and reward can be added to strengthen an already naturally high level of employee motivation.

The challenge of providing motivational management today is a significant one. Managers are struggling with changes and are actively engaged in a reinvention of management and indeed of work itself. This is an exciting time to be a manager. I hope the ideas and activities in this book have helped and will continue to help you as you make your own contribution to this exciting management journey.

*   *   *

Congratulations!

Well, you've done it. You've completed eleven challenging chapters and explored an important new approach to management. Your

understanding of your own and others' motivation and your ability
to boost motivation levels should be much greater now. I hope you
are excited about the possibilities, and the potential for higher levels of motivation and performance in every group of employees.
Most employees are rarely challenged to perform up to their full
potential, but I believe that if you take the time and care to apply
motivational management methods, you and your people will be
pleasantly surprised by the results.

Thanks for your interest and all the effort that went into reading
this book. I hope it is the beginning of a wonderful leadership journey for you and your employees!

Measuring and Tracking Job Motivation Levels

An appendix is normally not read at the time you read the rest of the book, but is referred to after you have read the book and its information is more useful. This appendix covers a tool and technique for tracking motivation levels, with motivation being defined, as in the book, as self-motivation with an emphasis on initiative and a high achievement orientation. In other words, the kind of motivation needed for the level-two economic environment described in the Introduction and Chapter 1.

Why measure motivation? If it is important to the achievement of your management goals, then it is probably something you want to quantify and track. Measuring anything is a prerequisite to managing it. Exercise 1-3 in Chapter 1 is a simple assessment for measuring the extent to which employees are *intrinsically* versus *extrinsically* motivated. You can use that to begin tracking the effect of your motivational management efforts. However, if you want to take it a bit further, this appendix offers another, more detailed tool. It also considers other ways of measuring and evaluating the level of work motivation in any group.

I have written this appendix just like I did the chapters. I don't want it to be dull or difficult to read, just because it's an appendix. If you want to explore the subject of measuring motivation in greater depth, jump right in and keep reading!

Creating Your Own Feedback System

The purpose of this book is to help you learn to manage for maximum motivation—and not just any old motivation, but intrinsic motivation, the kind that comes from within. In Exercise 1-1 in Chapter 1, you explored the characteristics of your ideal employee, someone with initiative, commitment, dedication, and drive, someone who does good work and does the right thing—often without your having to tell him or her what to do. This exercise creates a portrait of a highly motivated employee. It demonstrates the important point that motivational management can and should produce observable differences in employees. If it is working, this approach to management should produce employees who have visible levels of motivation. They look and act motivated. If not, then there is no point.

In this appendix, we are going to take the idea that motivation should be visible to a higher level. We are going to make employee motivation measurable, just like other things you manage for, like sales or profits or expenses. Why? Because it is very hard to manage anything if you can't measure and track it with a reasonable degree of accuracy. You need clear, accurate feedback about your efforts to use motivational management, just as your employees need good feedback about their work. So in the following pages we will discuss a simple and reasonably quick method of tracking employee motivation, which you can use to keep a running score. If the score goes up, you can correlate that improvement with something you did and do more of it. If the score goes down, you can see whether it is something you did and stop doing it. Or perhaps you will realize that an external event (like a layoff) has hurt morale and has driven motivation down, and you will know to step up your motivational management efforts for a while to compensate.

In short, by tracking the motivation level in your group of employees, you will be able to manage motivation in a more systematic manner. You won't always be guessing. You will instead be responding to information and reacting to observations. You will be working in a more feedback-rich environment than most managers do, and this will help you implement motivational management methods more easily and effectively.

Sighting the Target: What High Motivation Looks Like

One reason that businesses rarely measure employee motivation is that motivation isn't a simple, one-dimensional thing, like profit, for instance. Recall Exercise 1-1, in which you described your ideal employee. You probably listed multiple characteristics that together add up to your view of a highly motivated employee. So to measure motivation, it is necessary to look for multiple indicators. You can develop your own measurement method in which you rate how strongly your employees are exhibiting each of the characteristics you hope to see as a result of your motivational management efforts. Or, to simplify things a bit, you can use a generic approach that I developed, in which employees are evaluated according to the following seven measures, each of which is a good general indicator of their level of job motivation, and in particular of intrinsic motivation:

1. *Amount:* How much do they work?

2. *Effort:* How hard do they work?

3. *Focus:* How involved or caught up are they in work?

4. *Enjoyment:* How much do they enjoy doing their work?

5. *Intention:* Do they anticipate staying in the current job?

6. *Achievement:* Are they are performing at a high personal level?

7. *Volunteering:* Are they are eager to take on responsibilities?

So we can define highly motivated employees as employees who do a large amount of work, who put in a high degree of effort, who are highly focused on their work, who seem to enjoy their work and want to stick with it for the foreseeable future, who are producing good personal performances, and who are eager to step up and do whatever needs doing. Employees like this are winners who do their work exceptionally well, and who are therefore a joy to manage. So it makes sense to use these seven indicators to track employee motivation levels. You can think of them as good aspirational goals for you as a manager, because obviously most employees don't fit this definition of high motivation that well—at least to start with.

Using the Job Motivation Level Inventory to Give You Needed Feedback

Exhibit A-1 is the *management version* of the Job Motivation Level (JML) Inventory. It defines job motivation level as the sum of all seven of the characteristics we just reviewed. You can fill it in to measure how motivated your people are. Better yet, make a copy of it and fill in the copy, then you can use it again and again to track changes in motivation over time.

Benchmarking to Set Goals and Track Progress

The JML Inventory is a powerful tool for measuring and managing employee job motivation—which most organizations fail to measure or track. In general, employees operate at medium or low motivation levels, meaning that there is considerable performance potential that has not been tapped. Use the JML Inventory to identify and take advantage of any attitude-related performance gaps. Companies sometimes use a survey version of the JML Inventory to ask employees to measure their own motivation levels directly, but a simpler approach is for you, the manager, to fill in a JML Inventory based on your impressions of your employees. The version in Exhibit A-1 is designed for you to use this way.

You can use the JML Inventory to make regular measurements of your employees' attitudes toward their work. Tracking employee

(text continues on page 241)

EXHIBIT A-1. JML Inventory. ───────────────────────────

Job Motivation Level Inventory

This version is for managers to assess a group of employees they supervise.

Instructions

Here is the scale you should use as you select your answers and choose numbers to circle:

> 1 = very strongly disagree
> 2 = strongly disagree
> 3 = disagree
> 4 = neither disagree nor agree
> 5 = agree
> 6 = strongly agree
> 7 = very strongly agree

Now please go to the next page and fill it in by circling one (and only one) number for each of the 28 statements.

	Circle one
1. They are highly productive.	1 2 3 4 5 6 7
2. They put a lot of effort into their work.	1 2 3 4 5 6 7
3. Their work interests them.	1 2 3 4 5 6 7
4. For them, work is its own reward.	1 2 3 4 5 6 7
5. It is important to their careers to succeed in their jobs.	1 2 3 4 5 6 7
6. They are performing at very high levels right now.	1 2 3 4 5 6 7
7. They often volunteer to take care of things that need doing.	1 2 3 4 5 6 7

(continues)

EXHIBIT A-1. (Continued). ——————————————————

8. They work more than most people do.	1 2 3 4 5 6 7
9. They feel enthusiastic about doing their work.	1 2 3 4 5 6 7
10. They concentrate very hard on their work.	1 2 3 4 5 6 7
11. They really enjoy the work they are doing right now.	1 2 3 4 5 6 7
12. They are very content with their current jobs.	1 2 3 4 5 6 7
13. They are doing better work right now than they've ever done before.	1 2 3 4 5 6 7
14. They like to put in that extra effort that makes the difference between average and excellent work.	1 2 3 4 5 6 7
15. They put more time into their work than they have to.	1 2 3 4 5 6 7
16. They try harder to do a good job than most people do.	1 2 3 4 5 6 7
17. When they are working, they often lose track of time.	1 2 3 4 5 6 7
18. They are happy most of the time when they're at work.	1 2 3 4 5 6 7
19. They can't imagine doing anything else right now.	1 2 3 4 5 6 7
20. They are performing better than they thought they could.	1 2 3 4 5 6 7
21. They often help others out in order to make sure work is completed properly.	1 2 3 4 5 6 7
22. They rarely miss a day of work.	1 2 3 4 5 6 7
23. They try their best to do their jobs well.	1 2 3 4 5 6 7
24. When they are working, they tend to forget about everything else.	1 2 3 4 5 6 7
25. They feel good about their work.	1 2 3 4 5 6 7

26. Their current positions offer them opportunities to grow   1 2 3 4 5 6 7
professionally.

27. Their jobs give them opportunities to do exceptionally   1 2 3 4 5 6 7
good work.

28. They are not satisfied until the job is done to their own   1 2 3 4 5 6 7
personal standards of excellence.

Interpreting Your Results

The first step in interpreting the results of the JML is to summarize your results. Please transfer your scores to the following table.

Work across the rows, entering each of the numbers you circled in the order you circled it.

Score Form

Set: A	B	C	D	E	F	G
1: ____	2: ____	3: ____	4: ____	5: ____	6: ____	7: ____
8: ____	9: ____	10: ____	11: ____	12: ____	13: ____	14: ____
15: ____	16: ____	17: ____	18: ____	19: ____	20: ____	21: ____
22: ____	23: ____	24: ____	25: ____	26: ____	27: ____	28: ____
Totals ↓	↓	↓	↓	↓	↓	↓
Amount	Effort	Focus	Enjoyment	Intention	Achievement	Volunteering

Totals

Your totals on the bottom line of the table are called *component scores*. They measure components of the overall JML score. JML component scores can range from 4 (very low) to 28 (very high). Scores of 16 or less indicate seriously demotivated employees and suggest you have an urgent problem or perhaps multiple problems affecting employees and their job attitudes. Scores above 16 indicate some positive motivation on the part of employees. Scores over 20 indicate reasonably highly motivated employees—that is a good control limit below which you should not allow scores to fall if possible.

(continues)

EXHIBIT A-1. (Continued). ──────────────────

Definitions of Components

Each of your totals is a *component score,* telling you how your employees are doing in one of the seven components of overall job motivation. Motivation is not a simple, one-dimensional thing. It needs to be measured in multiple ways. The JML measures seven variables in order to provide a more accurate and realistic measure of overall job motivation level. Below, each of these components of motivation is defined.*

JML Component Table
and Form for Calculating Overall JML

Score?	Component	Definition
	Amount	How much they work
	Effort	How hard they work
	Focus	How involved or caught up they are in work
	Enjoyment	How much they enjoy doing their work
	Intention	Whether they anticipate staying in the current job
	Achievement	Whether they are performing at a high personal level
	Volunteering	Whether they are eager to take on responsibilities
	= Job Motivation Level	

Total?

*The JML measures components that are within the control of direct managers since it is designed for use in supervisory management. For company-wide measures of JML you may wish to include *commitment to the organization* as well. Contact us for a copy of the expanded Organizational JML Inventory.

Calculating Overall JML Score

You can easily calculate the overall Job Motivation Level by totaling the seven component scores. The possible range is 28 to 196. To help you interpret your score, the following bar chart shows you what the score means.

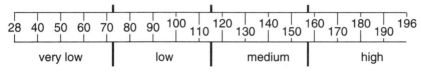

attitudes on a weekly or monthly basis is a very useful exercise. It makes it possible to manage attitudes. Typically, managers and their organizations do not keep track of or measure employee job attitudes, and as a result are not systematic about managing attitudes. And as we've seen in this book, attitudes are a powerful hidden component of employee performance and of overall organizational performance. Large-scale studies indicate that the attitudes measured by the JML Inventory control 40 to 50 percent of the variation of profits in business organizations. That means there is a very good bottom-line reason for managers to begin to measure and manage employee attitudes more systematically than they now do.

If you collect data using the JML form from Exhibit A-1 once every month, you should have pretty good data for your control chart.

It's also a good idea to keep a simple journal or log of the things you try and do in your efforts to boost employee motivation. That way, you can look back to see what you might have done in any past month to produce a positive or negative impact on your own and others' JML scores.

If you track and experiment with your own management behavior, and you measure the results in terms of employee motivation and business performance, you should begin to see these performance links more clearly than most managers do. You should feel increasingly in control of your bottom-line performance results as a manager, because the better you understand the links from your own behavior to your employees' behavior to your business results, the more easily you can control those results!

Treating Low JML Scores

Each of the seven JML components is a surface indicator of underlying job motivation level. With demotivated employees, component scores are good indicators of the demotivation problem—like symptoms of an underlying illness. When there is a motivation problem, then it will be reflected in one or more employee motivation symptoms, such as not working as much as they should or not working as hard as they could.

Different individuals have different symptoms to differing degrees—just as some people infected with a cold tend to get runny noses, while others get sore throats. So regardless of the specific symptoms of a motivation problem, managers need to respond by working on general motivation. You cannot cure an underlying motivation problem just by treating the symptoms.

However, it can be helpful to combine general motivational management as described in this book—the treatment of the underlying problem—with some specific treatments for specific components. When you find that one or two JML components are notably lower than the others, then you can use the following treatment suggestions to customize your approach to the problem.

Amount

When an employee or group is not putting in enough time on the job, you need to communicate your expectations clearly and often, and also to provide frequent feedback about the amount of work they do. For example, you might make an announcement or circulate a memo setting a goal of a 10 percent increase in how much each employee works, along with a reminder that they agreed to work at that level when they came on board. Then you could ask each employee to track their own amount of work daily to make them responsible for putting in the required time.

Once a week or once every two weeks, you could check with each employee face-to-face to see how they are doing on the goal. And if you think they are not keeping accurate records or not cooperating, you could share your own information about their performance at that time in order to make sure they understand how you view their performance on this dimension of JML Inventory.

Also, make sure you explain, clearly and frequently, why it is important for the company and for the employee to do the amount of work you wish them to do, and not to do less than you expect. If employees do not think their work is important, they often exhibit the symptom of doing less work than you want them to.

But remember that your ability to make progress with employees on this specific dimension of JML Inventory may be limited if there are underlying attitude problems or issues. Make sure employees have an appropriate level of challenge (neither too hard nor too easy). Make sure they feel they are being treated fairly. Make sure they have a positive emotional framework and feel that their managers and coworkers are considerate and friendly. And make sure they understand why their work is important and, in particular, *why it is important for them to do the amount of work you wish them to do*.

Effort

Effort is often closely related to amount, and it is common to find employees doing less work and putting less effort into the work they do. These symptoms indicate an underlying motivation problem, often one having to do with lack of appreciation for why the work is important. Make sure employees are aware that their work counts. Why does it make a difference whether they work hard or not? Explain this, and give them clear feedback to show that there are good results when they put in effort, and poor results when they don't.

Employees who are not putting in their best effort need to be encouraged too. Effort is closely related to optimism and enthusiasm. If employees are feeling a little down or discouraged—about work or about life in general—they will naturally slack off a bit in work. So sharing positive, can-do attitudes and styles of self-talk is important for this symptom. Also, showing how good it can feel to work hard and feel proud of your effort will help. Let employees see that you as a manager work hard and like to put your all into something when you are working.

And last but not least, praise hard work. Managers rarely recognize effort—it's much more common to praise good work than hard work. But if you make a point of mentioning it whenever you see someone working hard, you will encourage this behavior. In fact, the best way to stimulate hard work, even in someone who is not working very hard, is to thank them for their effort.

Focus

When focus is low, the employee is not "in the flow" and caught up in enjoyment of work. Most often, this is because of three likely causes. First, the work may not be challenging enough, in which case you can "raise the bar" by increasing the quality or quantity goals or by giving the employee responsibility for a larger, more visible chunk of the work flow. Second, the work may not seem important to the employee, in which case you need to share information and feelings that relate the work to important goals that the employee can get excited about. And third, the employee may not feel sufficiently skilled and confident to do the work well, in which case you can provide more support and coaching and make sure the information and resources needed to do the job well are available to the employee.

Enjoyment

When enjoyment scores are low, it means employees do not have much fun at work. Contrary to traditional management views, it is important to enjoy one's work. Enjoyment of work indicates that employees feel positive about what they do, get a sense of satisfaction from it, and enjoy the people they work with. To fix a low enjoyment score, make sure there are no underlying fundamental problems, such as poor communication with you, the manager, or conflicts with coworkers that aren't resolved cooperatively, or the perception of unfair treatment. Then work on raising positive feelings by being friendly (the more often you smile at employees, the more motivated they will be). Also use more recognition and rewards, because public recognition of accomplishment or even just of hard effort generally raises people's moods.

And give employees new opportunities to customize their workspaces (and if possible schedules too). The more control people feel they have over even the minute details of their work environment—lighting, location of furniture/equipment, personal belongings/decorations, sounds, temperature, etc.), the happier they are in that work environment. And in general, giving employees control over lots of little things boosts their optimism and motivation and encourages them to take initiative.

Intention

When you know that employees intend to leave their jobs soon, you need to work on retention right away. Every time you lose an employee, it makes others wonder if they should be leaving too, so departures have hidden costs throughout the work group. One good strategy for employees who are not very committed to their current jobs is to ask them in an open, interested way what they hope to get out of their work and where they want to be in the future. Find out what their personal aspirations are. Then see if you can help them pursue those goals right now, through their current work.

Often you as a manager can help employees gain specific kinds of experience that make them feel that they are moving toward their future goals. Anything you can do to help them with their own career and personal goals—even just showing interest—tends to make them feel more committed to their current job and more interested in sticking with it. Harness the power of motivational opportunities when you want to encourage employees to feel committed to sticking with their jobs.

Achievement

When the achievement score is low it indicates a serious issue that affects overall job motivation. The employees are not being challenged in a positive way, and therefore do not feel like they are performing well and demonstrating competence. You need to revisit their current work and job design, and look for lots of little ways to give them opportunities to succeed. Even if you have to make up simple, minor projects to give them, do so—any opportunities you can create for them to achieve will help get them reengaged with their natural need for achievement and the satisfaction that completing something worthwhile always brings.

Also make sure the relevance and importance of their work is obvious to them, and that they get lots and lots of feedback about how well they do it. Employees with low achievement scores often feel like they are playing a game in which the scores are not posted. Give them more detailed, accurate, and frequent information about how well they are doing. When they see they can control the scores through their actions, they will naturally want to improve those scores—and their achievement orientation will grow.

Volunteering

Some employees do their assigned tasks competently, but take no interest in any other work and show no initiative of their own. These employees receive low volunteering scores, and their co-workers resent that they are not "pulling their weight." They often duck responsibilities and say things like "that's not my department."

To fix this problem, look for underlying issues of fairness or resentment about how the employee has been treated. Employees with low volunteering scores often feel that they have been asked to do more than their share in the past, or that they have been treated unfairly. But rather than complain openly, they subconsciously withdraw from their work and no longer put their full effort into it. So try to open up the dialog with these employees. Share lots of information with them, and ask them to share their feelings and concerns with you.

Surprisingly, you can often fix this problem more "with honey than vinegar," so try being concerned and helpful to these employees. They will tend to reciprocate by being more helpful to others in the workplace. Also, make a point of praising them informally and personally (in a note, e-mail, or face-to-face) whenever they do take on responsibilities or show initiative or helpfulness. Perhaps they have not been recognized for volunteering in the past, and so, without positive reinforcement, are now avoiding the behavior.

The Smile Test

Ken Blanchard, the coauthor of *The One Minute Manager* and many other good books on management, likes to say that "feedback is the breakfast of champions." The JML Inventory is one form of feedback you can use to see how well your motivational management is going. It's a good method in part because it is informative—it puts a simple, repeatable measurement in front of you for you to use in tracking motivation level. (Keep in mind however that this measure is only partially controllable by you. There may be occasional events beyond your control that affect it, in which case you will need to compensate for these events. But that's okay if you remember that much of the time you can and do control the level of your employees' motivation.)

There are many other forms of feedback you can create for yourself to help you learn to be a better and better motivational manager. For example, you might use what I like to call the *smile test*.

The smile test is something I use as a consultant and trainer when I come into an organization for the first time, because it gives me a quick indication of the level of intrinsic motivation in the organization. Here is how it works (and it is truly as simple as its name implies):

▶ If lots of people are smiling as they work, then it is a very healthy environment where there are good levels of motivation to start with and where I know my job won't be too difficult.

- ▶ If I only see occasional smiles, then I know motivation levels are at half mast and I've got to bury the negative feelings and do some serious work to boost motivation higher. Some motivational management methods are needed for sure.

- ▶ And if there is hardly ever a smile, well, I'm not fooled. No matter how professional my hosts may be or how impressive the office or plant, I know that motivation is at an unhealthy low and I'm in for a long hard struggle. (Of course I don't mind long hard struggles when the end result will be that more and more people will smile at me, so I don't let a failed smile test get me down.)

The reason the smile test works is that people smile a lot when they are highly motivated—especially when they are intrinsically motivated. And this seems to be true across many cultures. Because when people are excited and motivated by their work, when they are "in the flow" and pursuing interesting challenges, they feel happy. They enjoy their work. They are energized, but not tense or stressed. And they find themselves enjoying the company of others who are pursuing their work with similarly healthy attitudes. So everyone tends to smile a lot. Which makes the smile test a remarkably powerful and simple form of feedback about employee motivation. It's not as systematic as more careful methods like the JML Inventory, but it certainly can give you quick, informal feedback every day and even every hour.

I've even seen some managers keep a "smile chart" in which they track their daily impression of how smiley their employees are. It's another feedback loop for them, another indicator of employee motivation. And by making motivation more visible, it makes their job of motivational management easier and more rewarding.

There really is nothing as rewarding to a manager as a group of employees whose enthusiasm and commitment is expressed in smiles and eagerness to tackle the next assignment!

Do You Have to Make Them Laugh?

By the way, having fun at work seems to be the hot new trend, and lots of books, Web sites, and magazine articles urge us as managers to introduce games, jokes, and clowning around into our workplaces. This is not such a bad idea, but don't forget that your core responsibility as a manager is to make sure your people are working well on tasks they find meaningful. And when you do, you will find there is plenty of natural enthusiasm and positive energy in the workplace, and you won't need to supplement it that often with jokes and nonwork-related play. Sure, a good laugh is a nice release, but there is no need to push it and try to become a comedian. (For instance, you might end up offending somebody when you run out of good jokes and have to resort to insulting or crude ones.)

Fun arises naturally when you have highly self-motivated employees. So keep an eye on the level of smiles, but don't worry if the office doesn't sound like a sitcom sound track. A calm buzz of work-focused energy and enthusiasm is what you want to tune your ear to. And it should be present more of the time as you implement the methods in this book and become a more proficient motivational manager.

Summary

As a motivational manager, you need informative feedback about your efforts to boost intrinsic motivation and inspire your people to perform exceptionally well. If you don't measure their level of motivation, then you are working in the dark. One good way to create an informative scoreboard for yourself is to fill in the Job Motivation Level (JML) Inventory (Exhibit A-1), a short questionnaire that breaks employee motivation down into seven separate factors and uses descriptive statements to represent each. The result of this exercise is seven separate scores, one for each of the JML components. These scores can be summed to get an overall score that gives you a good indicator of overall motivation level in your group of employees. You can keep track of this overall score from month to month and try to move it upward. You can also relate it to your efforts to use different motivational management techniques. It will give you feedback about the success of your efforts. But don't forget that other things can affect the score too. For instance, bad news may push the score down, leading you to apply more motivational management methods and bring it up again.

You can also focus on the one or two lowest component scores from the JML Inventory. These give you clues as to what the underlying causes of low motivation may be. Use all the scores to help you select the most appropriate motivational management actions for each of the seven components of the JML Inventory.

For a quicker and less formal indicator of how healthy motivation is in any group of employees, use the smile test. Plenty of smiles are an indicator of high self-motivation.

Learning Goals for Each Chapter

I have included Learning Goals for each chapter because in my workshops and courses I follow the discipline of training design that says one must first decide what one wants to teach—what participants would most benefit from learning—and then (and only then) go about designing the course. That way there is a meaningful focus and structure to the project. We can have fun, we can wander from the point on occasion to explore an interesting side issue—but with clear learning goals we will always manage to get the core job done in the end.

It's an important discipline to impose on me as an author, and it can also be helpful to you the reader by letting you know on the simplest level what I hope to communicate in each chapter. And yes, it is a lot like writing to an outline, except learning goals are not an outline of what I feel like talking about but more meaningfully of what I hope my readers will take away and use in their important work.

Some of the readers of this book may also be trainers or course developers, and for them this appendix will be especially helpful. With it, they can easily provide training (whether lectures or activities) based on specific chapters. If they wish to assign reading in this book, and then teach the material in a workshop or course, it will be helpful if the main learning points are already laid out for each chapter.

I've found with some of my earlier books that corporate trainers will contact me with questions about how to create a course based on the book. Well, this appendix is at least the beginning of an answer to that question, if it comes up with this book. (It is not the entire answer because a good workshop or course is more than good content. It also needs a good learning process, which is more than I can go into in this appendix. However, I don't mind fielding questions about how to teach these learning points if you are a professional with such questions in mind. You can always reach me through my firm's Web site, alexhiam.com, or at my Amherst, Massachusetts, main office.)

Chapter 1. The Quest for Star Performers

1. Define the employee behaviors needed to succeed in your organization's economic environment.

2. Distinguish between intrinsic and extrinsic motivation.

3. Determine whether employees are acting out of intrinsic or extrinsic motivations (in order to know when a motivational leadership action might be needed).

Chapter 2. Creating a Positive Performance Environment

1. Identify common habits and reactions that no longer serve your management needs.

2. Recognize that employees will respond differently to your management efforts depending on their emotional state.

3. Identify a range of new habits and reactions that serve your management objectives better.

4. Recognize the need to take charge of building and maintaining the momentum of your workplace.

Chapter 3. Rethinking Management Communications

1. Recognize the important role communication plays in motivating (or demotivating) employees.

2. Distinguish between functional and motivational communications with employees.

3. Use participative problem-solving to engage employees more fully in their work.

4. Transform functional communications to more motivational ones.

5. Use communications that stimulate employees to get more involved in their work.

Chapter 4. Using Motivational Communication Techniques

1. Distinguish between questions that motivate employees and those that irritate them.

2. Open a meaningful dialogue with an employee about an important aspect of his or her work.

3. Use open-ended questions and active and passive listening to generate high employee involvement.

4. Manage body language to encourage employee involvement and stimulate meaningful communications about work.

5. Stimulate employees to think critically and creatively about their work.

6. Find the time to communicate more openly with employees.

Chapter 5. Tackling the Feelings That Drive Performance

1. Recognize when employees are feeling negative about their work so you can take steps to make them feel more positive.

2. Recognize when employees are feeling inactive so you can take steps to give them more energy and move them to a more active frame of mind.

3. Act in a considerate manner toward employees to help them feel more positive about their work.

4. Help employees focus on compelling goals to give them more energy and make them more action-oriented.

5. Recognize the importance of maintaining a high level of positive feelings yourself, so that your positive attitude can spread to others.

Chapter 6. Providing Challenging Opportunities

1. Ask employees what they want to accomplish.

2. Recognize and take advantage of employee's natural urge to achieve meaningful objectives.

3. Make sure employees are doing work that has a clear *purpose*, that *interests* them, and that they have the *ability* to do well.

4. Articulate a big-picture goal worth pursuing.

5. Check and adjust the level of challenge to make sure no one has too much or too little.

Chapter 7. Using Feedback to Motivate

1. Distinguish between useful feedback and feedback that does not really help employees improve their performances.

2. Catch yourself giving controlling styles of feedback and switch over to more informative styles in order to maximize intrinsic motivation.

3. Be careful not to let employees get discouraged by too much negative feedback.

4. Know how to engage employees in participative design of informative feedback systems

5. Make sure every one of your employees has clear, accurate, and useful feedback so that they can tell how well they are doing as they pursue important goals and objectives.

Chapter 8. Eliminating Contaminants

1. Make sure you are giving your employees enough control to encourage them to take initiative.

2. Identify your own control habits so you can avoid overly controlling management behaviors.

3. Manage your own motivation to make sure you are positive and enthusiastic enough to motivate others.

4. Identify situations in which employees feel unfairly treated and manage them so as to keep them from losing motivation.

5. Demonstrate open questioning, active listening, and creative problem-solving skills to help your employees resolve their conflicts productively and prevent the conflicts from destroying motivation.

Chapter 9. Transforming Negative Attitudes

1. Recognize negative talk and identify ways in which it can damage employee motivation and performance.

2. Notice when employees are blindly accepting limits and boundaries so you can encourage them to consider ways around barriers.

3. Notice when employees are portraying themselves or others as helpless victims so you can encourage them to take charge of solving their problems.

4. Notice when employees are playing blame games and transform their negative talk into a discussion of how to learn from mistakes.

5. Protect yourself against anger and frustration by recognizing that the most common form of negative talk is to "trash the boss"—and that it can be transformed into positive talk using the techniques in this chapter.

Chapter 10. Appealing to Individual Motives

1. Avoid the misuse of incentives that do not appeal to the targeted employees.

2. Recognize the influence of life-stage and personality on work motives so as to be more aware of what each individual may need and want from their work.

3. Use the Incentive Profile to find out what your own dominant work motives are.

4. Use the Incentive Profile to find out what each of your employees' dominant work motives are—and see how they differ from each other's and your own.

5. Run participative discussions with employees to explore their work motives and come up with ways to match them better as you assign tasks and recognize their contributions.

Chapter 11. Using Recognition and Rewards

1. Recognize when recognition and reward tactics are appropriate and when they are not.

2. Develop creative ideas for employee recognition and rewards.

3. Match recognition and reward options to employees' top
   work motives to make sure they are appropriate.

4. Design recognition and reward systems that create high employee involvement.

5. Provide informal recognition and rewards in your daily interactions with employees.

Appendix A. Measuring and Tracking Job Motivation Levels

1. Measure the overall level of job motivation in your group of
   employees on an ongoing basis.

2. Use your measurement system as a source of feedback about
   your own performance as a motivational manager.

3. Use your measurement system as an indicator of the impact
   of external events that might damage motivation—and set
   goals for responding effectively to these events.

4. Target specific indicators of low motivation and use the most
   appropriate motivational management methods to raise
   them.

5. Tell quickly how self-motivated and enthusiastic a group of
   employees is, just by observing them.

A P P E N D I X   C

The Incentive Profile

The Incentive Profile (2002 Edition) ————————————————————
Employee Self-Assessment Version
(Please don't distribute this form to other managers for their use as it is a
commercial product of considerable value, protected by copyright laws.)

Please read the first statement carefully, then circle one of the numbers to show
how strongly you agree with it. Continue for the rest of the statements. *Use this
scale:*

Scale
1 = low agreement
2 =
3 =   *to* . . .
4 =
5 = high agreement

I. Self-Assessment

		Low				High
1.	I want to feel proud of the group I work with.	1	2	3	4	5
2.	I like opportunities to express myself in my work.	1	2	3	4	5
3.	I am highly motivated by a difficult challenge.	1	2	3	4	5
4.	It's a real honor to be part of a winning team.	1	2	3	4	5
5.	I want to make a unique contribution.	1	2	3	4	5
6.	I feel best when I've done something I didn't think was possible.	1	2	3	4	5
7.	I want to work for an organization that is highly respected and admired.	1	2	3	4	5
8.	I want to be recognized for my individuality.	1	2	3	4	5
9.	I want to be recognized for my achievements.	1	2	3	4	5
10.	I value stability.	1	2	3	4	5
11.	I'm interested in opportunities to develop my skills.	1	2	3	4	5
12.	My goal is to have as many new experiences as possible.	1	2	3	4	5

13. It is important to have a comfortable work situation.	1	2	3	4	5
14. Professional development is very important to me.	1	2	3	4	5
15. I think life should be an adventure.	1	2	3	4	5
16. I need to feel that my position is secure.	1	2	3	4	5
17. I am eager to grow and develop throughout my career.	1	2	3	4	5
18. I want my work to be exciting.	1	2	3	4	5
19. Good work should earn you special privileges.	1	2	3	4	5
20. I prefer to do work that I feel is highly meaningful.	1	2	3	4	5
21. I enjoy competitive games.	1	2	3	4	5
22. It feels good to be honored with special treatment.	1	2	3	4	5
23. I need to know that my efforts have made a real difference.	1	2	3	4	5
24. I'm a tough competitor.	1	2	3	4	5
25. People who excel in their work deserve to be given special status.	1	2	3	4	5
26. I need to do work that serves some higher purpose.	1	2	3	4	5
27. I like opportunities to win.	1	2	3	4	5

28.	I need to be given credit for the work I do.	1	2	3	4	5
29.	I like to know that my managers care how I feel.	1	2	3	4	5
30.	I want to have plenty of control over my own situation.	1	2	3	4	5
31.	It is a shame that good efforts are not always recognized by others.	1	2	3	4	5
32.	It is important for organizations to take good care of their members.	1	2	3	4	5
33.	I like to have plenty of options.	1	2	3	4	5
34.	People should always be thanked for their contributions.	1	2	3	4	5
35.	I work best in a supportive atmosphere.	1	2	3	4	5
36.	I prefer to control how and when I do my work.	1	2	3	4	5
37.	A significant reward is the best sign of appreciation for a job well done.	1	2	3	4	5
38.	I hope to play an increasingly important role in my work.	1	2	3	4	5
39.	I work primarily to take care of my personal needs.	1	2	3	4	5
40.	Employees who work hard should be given appropriately valuable rewards.	1	2	3	4	5
41.	I wish to achieve a position of greater trust and responsibility in the near future.	1	2	3	4	5

		1	2	3	4	5
42.	My family needs are my main concern at the moment.	1	2	3	4	5
43.	I am motivated by jobs that give you opportunities to achieve significant wealth.	1	2	3	4	5
44.	I am motivated to play a responsible leadership role in the workplace and in society as a whole.	1	2	3	4	5
45.	I want my employer to accommodate my important outside-of-work needs.	1	2	3	4	5

II. Understanding Your Reasons for Working

Which motivators are most important for you?
Which are least important?

To find out what your major motivators are based on your answers, please take a moment to fill in the table on the following page.

Record each of your scores in the appropriate blanks. The easiest way to do this is to simply enter the first three scores (numbers you circled), in order, from top to bottom in the first column. Now notice that the score form skips to the second column for answers 4, 5, and 6. Next, it skips to the third column for answers 7, 8, and 9. So you need to enter your scores in this sequence: Three down, skip up and across, three down, skip up and across, then back to the left and repeat the pattern:

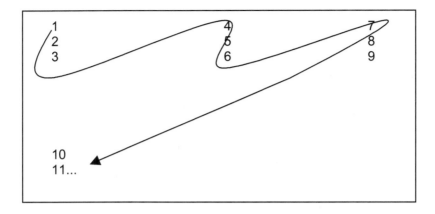

By entering the answers in this pattern you are "unscrambling" the survey and separating it into its fifteen sets of three statements—one set for each of fifteen different work motives.

Finally, **add each row**. Add left to right (not top to bottom). Each row has three scores for you to add, and your total for each row will be a number from 3 to 15. The higher it is, the more important the motivator listed at the end of that row is for you in your work.

Please enter your answers in the correct blanks below.

Then total each row to find your motivator scores.

Item	Your Score	Item	Your Score	Item	Your Score	Row Total =	Motivator
1		4		7			**Affiliation**
2		5		8			**Self-expression**
3		6		9			**Achievement**
10		13		16			**Security**
11		14		17			**Career Growth**
12		15		18			**Excitement**
19		22		25			**Status**
20		23		26			**Purpose**
21		24		27			**Competition**
28		31		34			**Recognition**
29		32		35			**Consideration**
30		33		36			**Autonomy**
37		40		43			**Rewards**
38		41		44			**Responsibility**
39		42		45			**Personal Needs**

III. Interpreting Your Results

When people have a clear understanding of what motivates them in their work they can make sure they are working toward their goals. It's easier to get what you want when you *know* what you want. Let's use your scores to gain a detailed understanding of the work motives that are most important to you right now.

Motivators Some of these 15 incentives are more important to you than others:	√ check if score is one of your three highest*	Definitions To gain a better understanding of your high-rated motivators, read their definitions below:
Affiliation		Feeling proud to be part of the group you work with. Pleasure in being associated with a great organization.
Self-Expression		Urge to express yourself individually and uniquely through your work.
Achievement		Drive to accomplish challenging goals. Pursuit of excellence.
Security		Need for stability or reduction of uncertainty and stress.
Career Growth		Urge to grow and develop in your career.
Excitement		Impulse to seek new experiences and enjoy life through your work.
Status		Motivation to increase your standing through your accomplishments.

Purpose		Need for meaning and direction. Desire for important work that really matters.
Competition		Competitive spirit. Desire to excel in relation to others.
Recognition		Need for positive feedback and support from the group. Desire to be appropriately recognized for your contributions.
Consideration		Preference for a friendly, supportive work environment where people take care of each other.
Autonomy		Need for more control over your own working life. Desire for choice of working conditions or other options.
Rewards		Motivation to earn significant rewards or wealth from one's work.
Responsibility		Motivation to play a responsible leadership role in the workplace or society as a whole.
Personal Needs		Need to satisfy important outside-of-work priorities.

*Most people have between one and three top scores. Some may have more, especially if there are ties.

Index